The Muckrakers

Waterloo Local Schools

The Muckrakers

CRUSADING JOURNALISTS WHO CHANGED AMERICA

Fred J. Cook

Doubleday & Company, Inc.
Garden City, New York

Contents

CHAPTER I

TR Coins a Phrase

PRESIDENT THEODORE ROOSEVELT, the beloved TR of reform, was speaking on April 14, 1906, before a group of politicians as rascally as any in American history—the members of the United States Senate.

The occasion was the laying of the cornerstone of the new House of Representatives Office Building in Washington, D.C., and the atmosphere was one of patriotism riding high. The area was draped with flags and bunting. Into a sealed copper box to be imbedded in the cornerstone went a copy of the Declaration of Independence, a copy of the Constitution, and a collection of American coins and stamps. The U. S. Marine Band played. Prayers were offered for the nation and its chief executive. Then the President spoke—and coined a phrase that has lived ever since in the language.

TR was in rare, fine form that day. His great white teeth flashed beneath his dark, bristling mustache; the sun glinted on his round rimless glasses; and his stocky body vibrated with earnestness as his powerful right arm and fist rose up and down in a thumping gesture.

The cause of the President's fury was a band of crusading journalists—the greatest, most skillful practitioners of the art of exposé the nation has ever known. For nearly four years, beginning in October 1902, these hard-digging writers had left no rock unturned. They had probed deep, and they had exposed the massive injustices and corruptions of an American society that, in its greed, had cast overboard all concepts of honor and most of the principles of true democratic government.

They had demonstrated that the huge corporations which were coming to dominate American life had been founded, not alone on hard work and vision and skill, but on ruthlessness, callousness, and bribery. They had shown how, in city after city, the police were the paid partners of the underworld. They had made the American public almost sick to its stomach by detailing how great packing houses packaged rats—and even unfortunate workers who happened to fall into their vats—into their meat products. They had discovered that even the most holy of churches owned whole blocks of the most foul and evil-smelling slums in the land, making huge profits out of human misery. And finally they had committed the sin of sins: they had attacked the mighty members of the U. S. Senate itself—a body of men who, almost without exception, had been purchased body and soul by the corrupt interests that were destroying the American dream; a body of men so corrupt

8

that hardly any of them recognized the odor of their own corruption.

It was too much. It was not to be borne. This final shaft of truth lighting up the seamy American landscape had gored the politicians of the day in their most sensitive spot; and now even the great TR, the apostle of the Square Deal and reform, felt impelled to defend the corrupted against those who had exposed their corruption.

Theodore Roosevelt's image with the public was that of a crusader for right and justice. To an extent, he was. But it was also true that his reforming zeal was always limited, always subordinated to practical political purposes. He was the President, but he had to work with the Senate. To get even watered-down reform measures enacted into law, he had to bargain, he had to twist some reluctant arms, he had to deal with the very members of a legislative body beholden to the powers he was attempting to reform. And how could he be expected to continue to deal with them unless he defended their non-existent honor?

They sat there looking up at him as he spoke—the man most of them either disliked, distrusted, or even positively hated; the man who was now, from the necessities of politics, their champion. According to one account of the day, the seating scheme was such that "the Senate was literally at the President's feet and the executive could have reached over the rail of the speaker's stand and touched the heads" of Senate leaders who occupied "the front pew."

After a brief introductory paragraph, Roosevelt—for all the world like the Rough Rider who had led his troops up San Juan Hill in the Spanish-American War—charged headlong at the band of crusading journalists who had dared to expose even the sacred U. S. Senate. He thundered:

9

"In Bunyan's *Pilgrim's Progress* you may recall the description of the Man with the Muckrake, the man who could look no way but downward, with a muckrake in his hands; who was offered a celestial crown for his muckrake, but who would neither look up nor regard the crown he was offered, but continued to rake to himself the filth of the floor.

"In *Pilgrim's Progress* the Man with the Muckrake is set forth as an example of him whose vision is fixed on carnal instead of on spiritual things. Yet he also typifies the man who in this life consistently refuses to see aught that is lofty, and fixes his eyes with solemn intentness only on that which is vile and debasing. Now, it is very necessary that we should not flinch from seeing what is vile and debasing. There is filth on the floor, and it must be scraped up with the muckrake; and there are times and places where this service is the most needed of all the services that can be performed. But the man who never does anything else, who never thinks or speaks or writes save of his feats with the muckrake, speedily becomes, not a help to society, not an incitement to good, but one of the most potent forces of evil."

With these words the President labeled all of the crusading journalists of the day muckrakers. It was a term that stuck. The conservative press and the forces of corruption that the muckrakers had attacked leaped on the term with glee, deriding and belittling the stream of documented exposés which had so aroused the American people and had shaken the nation to its foundations.

But what neither TR nor the power brokers of the nation had anticipated was that the muckrakers would also seize upon the label and apply it to themselves as a badge of honor. They had become so important that they had been attacked by the President himself; and what was more, as some of them delighted in pointing out, TR had been so carried away in attacking them that he had gotten his references all backward. Bunyan in *Pilgrim's Progress* had applied the term muckraker in an entirely different way; he had pictured the muckraker as the man who wastes his whole life raking in the muck for money—the very type of man the muckrakers were attacking and exposing.

This vital difference in meaning could hardly be expected, however, to register with the public. The public took Roosevelt's words as they had been intended, and to many the label muckraker became an epithet. And so in the end this biting phrase did its damage.

The muckrakers were subjected to ridicule, to a barrage of attacks, to all kinds of financial pressures—a combination which, in another six years, would overwhelm and doom a journalistic movement unique in our history. There had never been anything like it before; there has never been anything like it since; and there can probably never be anything like it ever again.

But in the ten years that the muckrakers flourished, from 1902 to 1912, they represented a novel and powerful force. They gave voice to deep-seated and long-lasting anxieties, grievances, and suspicions of the American public. And they certainly helped to make possible the great wave of progressive reform that marked the first sixteen years of the century. In a word, they changed things. And not many writers can ever claim to have done that.

CHAPTER II

The America of the Muckrakers

THE MUCKRAKERS succeeded for so long because the climate of America was ripe for exposure. The thirty-five years from the end of the Civil War to 1900 had seen the vast reaches of a magnificent continent looted on a scale unrivaled in the history of human greed. It was a looting made possible by use of brute force, by the devious throat-cutting of business rivals, by an almost universal system of bribery and corruption.

The Civil War had been the pivot of the new age. The planter aristocracy of the South, representing the elite of the rural society which had virtually run the nation from the days of Washington, had been crushed. And so the war it had sought, to preserve its control of the affairs of state, had ended with the enthronement of its hated rivals, the industrialists of the North.

A successful war always enriches the rich, and the Civil War was no exception. The financial and industrial barons of the North, who had furnished war material to the government at exorbitant prices, came out of the conflict, rolling in a wealth beyond their fondest dreams. And there before them, waiting to be exploited, lay the whole vast, incredibly rich, undeveloped West stretching from the prairies to the Pacific.

In 1860 more than half of the entire nation—1,048,111,608 acres—belonged to the federal government. It was an acreage rich beyond the dreams of ordinary men. One-third of the land was covered by magnificent forests containing every kind of wood needed for industrial or domestic purposes. Below the surface lay treasures in coal and oil, and, in the wild West, whose resources were only now being discovered, were copper, gold, and silver mines worth the ransom of many kings. These were national treasures which the national government gave away for a song—or, indeed, for nothing—to those who had the capital to pull the right political strings.

Mining, lumber, and railroad interests, backed by the enormous capital accumulated during the war, stole or acquired with only a faint pretense of legality lands and riches equal to the wealth of many entire nations. The railroad industry alone was granted in the brief space of twenty-five years more than 150,000,000 acres of public land. This was an area equal in size to Maine, New Hampshire, Vermont, Massachusetts, Rhode Island, Connecticut, and New York, with a nice fat chunk of Pennsylvania thrown in for good measure.

The new emperors of business and finance who gorged themselves on a continent's wealth were, almost without exception, men of limited education. They had, as Theodore Roosevelt was to write with contempt, little vision or wisdom regarding the nation's needs. Their eyesight was limited largely to the black ink of their own ledgers. But when it came to acquiring this black ink, they had courage, drive, ruthlessness, cunning—and appetites that were never satisfied, no matter how many millions they possessed. It was little wonder that they became known as "the Robber Barons."

Here are the names of some of these new barons and their principalities: Jay Gould, William H. Vanderbilt, Collis P. Huntington, James J. Hill, and Edward H. Harriman—railroads; John D. Rockefeller—oil; Andrew Carnegie—steel; Jay Cooke and J. Pierpont Morgan—banking and finance; William A. Clark—mining; and Philip D. Armour—meatpacking.

It was notable, perhaps, that none of them had felt so driven by patriotism as to join the Union ranks during the Civil War. Two could not have. Harriman was only thirteen at the time, and Hill had defective eyesight. But the others, with no such valid excuses, simply went about the business of making money. Armour, for example, laid the foundation for his great fortune in a stock market killing. He sold pork "short" at just the right time—at the precise moment Union armies were driving through the Wilderness to end the Civil War.

In any event, it was these men and others like them, favored by state legislatures they bought and controlled, blessed by a national government that did their bidding, who changed the face of America in the short span of thirty-five years. They flung great rail networks across the nation from coast to coast; their mines disgorged incredible wealth; their factories belched forth smoke and steel; their oil pipelines and refineries opened up an entirely new industry, capable of turning millionaires into billionaires. Almost overnight, the nation was transformed from a largely rural and agricultural economy to an industrialized state. In 1870, the United States trailed both England and France in its output of iron and steel. Just twenty years later it had surpassed both of them and was producing one-third of the entire world's annual supply. The small mill on the riverbank, the family-owned medium-sized factory had been swept into the discard in those twenty years, and huge corporations, backed by massive financial power, had taken over and crushed all opposition. The new giants of business and their combinations had made America by 1890 the foremost manufacturing nation in the world.

This was the achievement. Americans for a time marveled at it, and few attempted to assess the cost. Yet costs there were—heavy costs to the very processes of American life and government. The historian Charles A. Beard later summed up in these words:

". . . Here is a chronicle of highly irregular and sometimes lawless methods, ruthless competition, menacing intrigues, and pitiless destruction of rivals. Private companies organize armed guards and wage pitched battles over the possession of rights of way for pipelines. Men ordinarily honest are seen slinking about in the cover of night to destroy property and intimidate persons who refuse to obey their orders . . . Newspapers are purchased; editors are hired to carry on propaganda and to traduce respectable citizens whose sole offense is the desire to handle an independent business . . ."

All this was only part of the cost.

The lightning-like expansion of American industry was fueled by two policies that complemented each other to the benefit of the robber barons. High protective tariff walls were erected. These freed American manufacturers from foreign competition; made possible fantastic, exorbitant profits—and, too, forced the great mass of American consumers to pay far more than they would otherwise have had to pay for the goods they consumed. Reaping such a bonanza on the one hand, the new industrial classes benefited on the other from an immigration policy that assured them plenty of cheap labor. Western Europeans, impoverished in their homelands or suffering from political persecution, emigrated to America by the millions. Ignorant, unskilled, not knowing the country or in many cases even the language, they became the ideal human fodder for the great smoking mills of the new industrial society. They helped to make possible the gigantic expansion which saw America accomplishing in thirty-five years an industrial revolution that had taken other nations centuries. But the human costs could never be calculated.

The new immigrants were herded together in the great manufacturing cities. They stewed in noisome slums. They worked killingly long hours for starvation wages. They lived in conditions of squalor and degradation that make one shudder today, just reading the muckrakers' descriptions of them. Inevitably, disease festered and lives were short. Drunkenness, vice, and crime flourished.

And this was only the initial entry on the debit side of the ledger. The immigrants were not the only victims. It took a little longer, but soon and inevitably the time came when native-born Americans, free men who had felt a

17

heady new independence in tilling their own soil, began to suffer even as the immigrants suffered.

In the past there had always been a new frontier to explore, new lands to acquire and till; there had always been an escape hatch beyond the prairies or the mountains for those overwhelmed by increasing pressures back East. But by 1900 the nation had been settled from coast to coast; the great national treasury of free land and forest had been squandered. There was no place else to go; and the costs, the problems, which had not seemed to matter so much before, could not be put off beyond a new horizon. They had to be faced and dealt with.

The result was upheaval. A one-sided system which had favored the new monarchs of business to the exclusion of all other classes began to take its toll. The great farming class, for generations the backbone of the nation, became a pitiful victim of the new society. Farmers had to sell their products in an unprotected, free-world market, but all the manufactured articles they had to buy were jacked up in price by the high protective tariffs. They also played the role of medieval serfs to the new dukes and counts of the railroad empire. The railroads, uncontrolled and unsupervised, charged whatever outrageous rates they estimated in their greed that the traffic could bear. Frequently, they charged as much to ship wheat as the wheat itself was worth. Railroads and middlemen who operated warehouses and grain storage elevators were frequently in cahoots; and, if railroad shipping charges did not rob the farmer of all profit, the storage half of the combine made certain it grabbed all that was left.

Even this was not the sum total of the farmer's miseries. To get his land and necessary equipment, to get his seed and finance his planting, he had to borrow. And his only source of money was that Eastern financial class protected by the government it controlled. Loans were pressed upon the farmer in good times at from 8 to 12 per cent interest; but these charges, much like the monthly rates assessed on today's easy-charge loans, were often hiked by indirection until they totaled 30 or 40 per cent annually. So squeezed and victimized on every side, farmers were ruined by the millions.

One farm spokesman put it this way:

"We went to work and plowed and planted; the rains fell, the sun shone, nature smiled, and we raised the big crop that they told us to; and what came of it? Eight cent corn, ten cent oats, two cent beef and no price at all for butter and eggs—that's what came of it . . ."

When depressions came—and they came every few years, sometimes touched off by the wild stock market speculations of the ruling classes—the Eastern mortgage companies foreclosed and booted the farmers off their hard-worked lands. When the panic of 1893 struck, more than 11,000 farm mortgages were foreclosed in Kansas alone, and two years later it was estimated that, in fifteen counties in that state, loan companies owned from 75 to 90 per cent of the land.

This, then, was the developing situation: while the moneyed men rode high, protected on every hand by state legislatures and a national government they controlled, millions of Americans were being crushed between the grindstones of an inequitable system—and were being driven to desperation. Factory workers who tried to organize unions in their battle for a living wage were attacked by hired thugs, brutally beaten and sometimes killed. Immigrants dragged out their short, miserable, hard-driven lives

19

in festering slums. And farmers, usually the most conservative class in the nation, began to talk like the French before they stormed the Bastille.

In 1890 farmers from the West and the Border States held a great rally in Topeka, Kansas, and formed a new political party that became known as the People's, or the Populist, Party. The mood of the convention was like that of a religious revival meeting; the hall jumped with fervor and passion and heated oratory. A star of the show was Mrs. Mary Ellen Lease, a handsome and distinguished woman, who shocked the Victorian sensibilities of the East by telling the farmers: "What you farmers need to do is to raise less corn and more *Hell!*" A lady simply didn't say "Hell" in those days.

This was, however, only Mrs. Lease's opening blast. She poured it on in these words:

"Wall Street owns the country. It is no longer a government of the people, by the people and for the people, but a government of Wall Street, by Wall Street and for Wall Street. The great common people of this country are slaves, and monopoly is the master . . . Our laws are the output of a system which clothes rascals in robes and honesty in rags. The parties lie to us and the political speakers mislead us . . . the politicians said we suffered from overproduction. Overproduction when 10,000 little children, so statistics tell us, starve to death every year in the United States, and over 100,000 shopgirls in New York are forced to sell their virtue for the bread their niggardly wages deny them!"

Whipped on by this kind of oratory, the Populist Party lighted a fire at the grass roots. It demanded free coinage of silver to put more money into circulation. It demanded regulation of the railroads, a graduated income tax to make the wealthy pay their proper share of the costs of government, a shorter work week for urban laborers (working hours were then practically unlimited), and the popular election of United States Senators, then chosen by the senates of boss-controlled legislatures. None of this program seems so very radical today, but the nation's Establishment at the time was shocked and horrified. And it was thrown into panic in the presidential election of 1892 when the Populists rolled up nearly one million votes for their little-known candidate, James B. Weaver of Iowa. Weaver actually carried some of the farm states and registered 22 votes in the Electoral College, the first time such a thing had happened since the days of Abraham Lincoln.

The political rebellion of the Populists was followed by the crash of 1893, and the nation seethed in a wild ferment caused by wrongs unrecognized and unrighted. In the spring of 1894, the conservative classes became hagridden by the fear that the nation was about to see the American version of the French Revolution, with heads rolling from the guillotine. Riotus hordes of desperate men gathered in the West, looted for food, seized railroad trains, and rode or marched toward the Eastern cities. In Los Angeles one thousand men were said to have joined such a robber-train band; in San Francisco, the figure was put at 2000; in Ohio, protest leaders claimed to be marshaling 150,000 men for a march on Washington.

U. S. Marshals were called out by the thousands. They pursued "lost" trains up and down the fastnesses of the Rocky Mountains; they fought some pitched battles with the protestors; they broke up and disbanded marching armies of the unemployed and desperate. Only some 250 to 300 Midwest protestors, legionnaires led by "General" Jacob

S. Coxey, actually got as far as Washington. There, as was to happen to Vietnam War protestors in Chicago in 1968, they were refused the right to march and demonstrate. Defying the ban, they straggled down Pennsylvania Avenue, their bagpipes skirling, until they were confronted by armed ranks blocking them off from the Capitol, where they had hoped to petition federal legislators to right their wrongs. Coxey and two of his followers dodged through the lines and tried to reach the Capitol, but they were ridden down, beaten, captured. When most of the watching crowd of 15,000 to 20,000 that lined the sidewalks cheered for Coxey and shouted at his captors, mounted police went berserk charging the crowd, swinging their clubs and beating or trampling down more than fifty persons.

Coxey's Army had been dispersed with such ridiculous ease that the nation's relieved Establishment laughed at its former fears. But the sufferings, the wrongs, the injustices—and the passions they aroused—remained. They waited for the muckrakers to paint them in their true colors.

CHAPTER III

"Cigarette"

THE MAN who put the word "graft" into the language deserves to be remembered as the first muckraker. It was his misfortune that he came a few years too soon, writing before the great wave of exposé journalism swept the nation, and so he is today unknown, his contribution forgotten. Yet the effects of his work and the name he gave to official corruption live with us still.

He was Josiah Flynt Willard, a man who combined in his person many characteristics of the muckrakers, but who lived a life uniquely his own, unlike any of the others. Like many of the other muckrakers, he was the child of wealth and secure social position; he had all the benefits of education; his background was that of sound, sober, well-to-do middle America. Unlike other muckrakers, however, he deliberately chose the life of a bum; and, from his boyhood to the day he died, he switched back and forth, at home in two distinctly different worlds—now circulating in the best of circles, now going "on the road" and making himself one with the dregs of the criminal underworld.

Born in Chicago in 1869, Josiah Willard was the son of the wealthy editor of a Chicago newspaper. His aunt was Frances Willard, a temperance leader and well-known feminist. From infancy, the boy was wrapped in the warmth and luxury of a home that possessed all the advantages of the day, but he early demonstrated his preference for an entirely different kind of life.

He was a small boy, short of stature, slightly built, but he was handsome, highly intelligent, and, above all, adventurous. He was little more than a child when he began to run away from home. "Running away" was something of a fad among boys in those days; there was a Huck Finn romanticism and adventuresomeness about it. But most boys who tried it quickly found that they could get pretty cold, hungry, and lonesome; that life at home was, after all, much more comfortable.

Not so Josiah Willard. He would take off, be gone for days, return for a short time—and then vanish again. In his roamings, he early discovered the threat—and perhaps, to him, the spice—of real danger. The industrial revolution which was making America a great power was already taking its toll. In the 1880s the number of unemployed doubled; the desperate and the lawless took to the highways; tramps, or "hobos" as they were called, became common and were to remain a fixture of American life well into the twentieth century.

Many of these hobos were not beloved "knights of the road," possessing hearts of gold under their rags. Many were savage and evil men. They hopped freight trains and rode from one end of the country to the other. Trainmen who tried to put them off were frequently fallen upon by a human wolf pack and savagely beaten, sometimes literally torn to pieces.

Such were the kinds of men with whom Josiah Willard associated at an early age. He was a born actor and mimic. On the spur of the moment, he could put himself into the role the moment required, and he would act out his part so convincingly that it seemed he must, indeed, be the person he was portraying. All of this skill was needed at times to save him. Time and again, his life was threatened by vicious tramps who suspected he did not "belong" or who simply took a dislike to his small, slight person. Time and again, Josiah's quick wits saved him as he talked his way out of difficult situations.

His comfortably situated family was naturally worried; the neighbors were horrified. When Josiah would return home, scrub himself up and go off to school like any other schoolboy, the neighbors would shake their heads, mutter that he was "a bad one," and prophesy that he would come to no good end. The Willards were possessed by the same fear, and they did everything they could think of to break their wayward son of his wandering habits.

They sent him off to the country to live with friendly relatives, hoping the joys of farm life would change him. They tried to understand him, to find reasons for his wander-lust; they tried to get him to promise to be good; they kept a close eye on him. Nothing worked. Josiah's home life was happy enough; he would seem perfectly contented for a time—and then, one day, he would be gone.

Why? It was a question no one could answer, not even

Josiah himself. In his autobiography, written after he had become a well-known author, he tried to explain, but he could not. There was just "something" that drew him to the Beyond, he said; he had to keep seeing new places, he had to keep meeting new people and he had to keep trying to find out what they were really like, stripped of all conventions. This curiosity was doubtless part of the force that drove him, but somewhere deeper down there had to be a more powerful and compelling motive for Josiah's fascination with the dregs of society.

In any event, despite this haphazard kind of boyhood, Josiah finally finished secondary school and went off to an Illinois college. Academic life, however, bored him. He found it pale and unreal compared to the "life of the road," and so he was soon off again, bumming it. This time, he made the mistake of stealing a gig; he was caught, arrested, and thrown into reform school. It was a school so bestial that it needed reform as badly as its inmates, and Josiah's experience in it was enough to shock him for a time into good behavior.

He gave regular living a whirl, studied, and decided he would go to Europe and enroll in the University of Berlin. German education was thought to be the best in the world at that time; and since Josiah came from a moneyed family, expense was no bar. Hoping that he had finally reformed, his worried parents were glad to send him off to Germany to see what "the best" could do for him. It soon became clear, however, that not even the challenge of a German university could hold Josiah. The wander bug soon bit him again and he was off, bumming it through Europe as he had through America without money, without clothes except those on his back, constantly in the company of thieves and tramps.

He shifted as always back and forth between two worlds. As a tramp, he became a familiar figure in all the slums of Germany, France, Russia, Italy, and Switzerland. As the son of distinguished American parents, he mingled when he chose with the upper levels of society, meeting some of the most distinguished men of his day. He talked with Ibsen and Tolstoy; he visited with famous journalists; and in London he became acquainted with the man who was to have the greatest influence on him, Arthur Symons, already a famous stylist.

Never were two men less alike. Symons was the lover of words, an intellectual, at home in the foremost literary and artistic circles of his day. Josiah Flynt, as he had now begun to call himself, dropping the family name of Willard, was small and gnomelike, possessed of quick intelligence, but no worshiper of the famous or the intellectual. His interest was the raw stuff of life—and the more raw, the better. As the friend of Symons, he met some of the major artistic and literary figures of the day, men such as Oscar Wilde and Aubrey Beardsley. But in his own and more natural role of the wandering bum, he was known in half the slums of Europe as "Cigarette."

Nothing pleased Josiah Flynt more than to take a party of society men and women down into the slums, showing them off to the bums with whom he rubbed shoulders. The socialites went, as they always do on such excursions, for the novelty and excitement of it, and Flynt got his kicks from being the central figure in both the worlds in which he was known. Many of his upperworld friends later marveled at his performance on such occasions. It was worthy, they vowed, of the best actors on the stage. In seconds he would change into an entirely different figure right before their eyes. By a change of gait, a different movement of hands and eyes, language that lapsed easily into the argot of the slums, he would be transformed from a society figure into a bum, the comrade of those who lived in the lowest dives. The slum rats, in turn, accepted such conducted tours by "Cigarette" with the hard-boiled attitude of the underworld. They assumed that their fellow traveler had picked up some society suckers whom he intended to fleece at the proper time.

It was a double life beyond the capacities of most men, but Josiah Flynt, having trained himself from boyhood, carried off the dual roles with baffling ease. His wanderings obviously had provided him with a gold mine of material and so, encouraged by Arthur Symons, he began to write. He was only twenty-five when his first sketches began to appear in 1894 in such magazines as the *Century*, the *Forum*, and the *Atlantic*. They dealt with tramp life as he knew it, and they broke sharply with the literary vogue of the day.

This was an era in which the popular novel, after entanglements and misunderstandings that kept the hero and heroine apart for hundreds of pages, built up to the great climactic scene at the end—the exchange of the first kiss. It was an era in which style was considered more important than content, and flowery verbiage and intricate sentence structure were hailed as proof of the writer's skill. Into such a world, divorced from the grim realities of life, came the work of Josiah Flynt.

He was no stylist. His writing was spare, devoid of flourishes, but it flowed naturally and easily. It was clear, swift-moving, and it dealt with the stuff of life as lived at the lowest levels. The staid Victorian world knew not what to make of it. When his first sketches were collected in book form under the title *Tramping with Tramps,* Flynt became famous overnight, but literary circles of the day shook their heads over him just as neighbors had once done at the boy in Chicago. Hardest for most people to accept was Flynt's discovery that there were all kinds and degrees of tramps. Society had considered all tramps automatically thieves and villains. Flynt portrayed the thieves and villains, but he also showed that there were other kinds of tramps—harmless, roaming, even likable creatures who had chosen the life of the vagabond as their way of life because (unthinkable thought) they liked it.

The success of Flynt's first book did not change his life pattern. Where another might have basked in the glow of fame, Flynt remained "Cigarette." He continued to go off on his underworld adventures. Though this period of his life is more shadowy than some others, he seems to have worked at times with police, helping to track down criminals, and he also put in a stint as a railroad policeman, covering as he said "a beat" 2000 miles long.

The life he had lived was now beginning to take its toll. In his impersonation of "Cigarette," he had to do the things the role called for; he had to live as his fellow vagabonds lived. He had to drink; he had to be one of the boys when drugs were being used. By 1900, at the age of thirty-one, Josiah Flynt was beginning to realize that he could not continue with this kind of life forever, and so he went to the most unusual magazine publisher of the day with an unusual proposition.

S. S. McClure was the publisher. He was an Irishman

who bubbled over with ideas, enthusiasm, and energy. McClure had struggled through a poverty-stricken boyhood, fighting his way up as he later said like a man trapped in quicksand. He had finally found a benefactor, Colonel Albert A. Pope, the founder of the Pope Manufacturing Company which made the Columbia bicycle. Pope made McClure editor of *The Wheelman,* later combined with *Outing.*

It was a secure job, but McClure was restless, driven. He could not work long for anyone else, no matter how good the job or the employer. Soon he decided to embark on a career of his own. He conceived the idea for a national syndicate which would reprint articles and stories and distribute them to newspapers across the country. He aimed at gaining a mass audience for the material he marketed.

It was a novel idea, something no one else had yet attempted, and McClure's syndicate struggled, almost died. But its determined, furiously working founder plugged it all over the nation, and finally it caught on. McClure began to make money. And as he did, his ideas took wing. He would establish a new, cheap, mass-circulation magazine.

Magazines in 1893 when McClure pounced on this new idea were priced at from 25 to 35 cents an issue—this in an era when a man might work from fifty to sixty hours a week for little more than $1 a day. Such workers obviously could not afford a 25-cent or 35-cent magazine. Here was a mass audience which was being neglected. McClure decided to take advantage of new developments in photoengraving and printing and to bring out a monthly magazine that almost everybody could afford, one that would sell for 15 cents an issue.

McClure's Magazine, like the syndicate before it, almost

strangled at birth. But McClure supported the magazine with revenue the syndicate was now earning, and it began to succeed. The reason for its growing success was, of course, the boundless enthusiasm of McClure himself. He bounced all around the country and went off on repeated trips to Europe, seeking new writers, new ideas. His enthusiasm often ran away with him. Time and again, he would fall for some utterly preposterous suggestion, welcoming it as a world-beater; and, when this happened, his editors back in New York would have to try to get him out of the pickle he had created. In this way, McClure might take up half-a-dozen ideas that even he could see were crackpot, once the heat of the moment had passed; but at the same time, for every half-dozen that had to be discarded, he would come up with one that was truly brilliant, a real winner.

Such was the publisher whom Josiah Flynt approached in 1900 with a suggestion that he do something that had never been attempted before. While bumming it in the Washington Square area of New York's Greenwich Village, Flynt had met Alfred Hodder. Hodder was slightly older than Flynt, a university graduate, and a writer who was concerned with the problems of reform. Flynt and Hodder, combining their talents, proposed to write a series of articles about the underworld that would tell it the way it was. Flynt took the idea to McClure, and that bouncy, ever-eager publisher welcomed it.

The series began to run in *McClure's* in August 1900 under the title "True Stories from the Underworld." In introducing the series, McClure stressed that the writers "have spent many years among criminals and are known amongst the 'profession' as men of their own class." Names had been changed, but the stories were true, McClure assured his

31

readers, and their importance was that "they are philosophical studies, about a class concerning which the great mass of people know nothing, except that they are law-breakers."

This was true. New York had been rudely shaken a few years previously by the great Lexow investigation that had proved widespread police corruption. The idea that gambling and prostitution existed because police were paid off to permit wide-open violations of the law had shocked New Yorkers at the time, but there had been little realization or acceptance of a cardinal fact: *that this was the way the system worked*, that the conditions exposed by the Lexow probe were not really unusual, but on the contrary quite common. The articles by Flynt and Hodder emphasized this startling concept.

Flynt was now at the height of his powers. The *McClure's* articles were collected into a book, *The Powers That Prey*. And this was followed by another, *Notes of an Itinerant Policeman*. In this, Flynt attempted to show that the policing of a great city was far more difficult than most persons imagined. The very nature of police work meant that the police had to have connections with the criminal class. They had to get information; they couldn't get it unless they themselves associated with criminals, cultivated informers—and offered some kind of reward for information received. The reformers' cries that crime should be "wiped out" were unrealistic, Flynt thought. The best that could be hoped for was that police forces could be made "cleaner" and "dishonest public servants" eliminated so that the police would be subject to more public control. All of this, of course, presupposed that the public itself really wanted to put an end to corruption, and this was something about which Flynt and his underworld cohorts had their doubts.

In these articles and books, Flynt was building up to his masterwork. In 1901, just a year after "True Stories from the Underworld" had appeared in *McClure's,* he started another series. It was called "The World of Graft"; it was based on Flynt's in-depth, face-to-face interviews with criminals in three major cities—New York, Chicago, and Boston; and it brought home to readers with shattering force the reality of underworld life and the long reach of corruption.

"Graft" was then a virtually unknown word; Flynt was to make it an everyday term in the language. As Flynt explained in an introduction when his *McClure's* articles were published in book form, the word "graft" was used in the underworld as a "slang term for all kinds of theft and illegal practices generally." Thus, thieves and thugs described themselves as "grafters"; they also referred to crooked politicians, policemen, and judges as "grafters." They distinguished between the upperworld and underworld grafters in this way: the criminal was called a "mugged grafter," meaning that his picture had been taken by police and was in rogues gallery files; the eminent officials who were taking bribes from the underworld were known as "unmugged grafters" since one wouldn't find their likenesses in any rogues gallery.

Flynt spent three springtime months bumming around the underworlds of the big cities on which he concentrated, and he gave his public a hard-eyed, realistic view of American society as seen from the bottom of the ant heap. He introduced a number of underworld slang phrases into his report besides "graft." The hardened criminal class was known as "the guns." Gangs were "mobs"; pickpockets were "dips"; an arrest was a "pinch"; disorderly houses or illegal

33

liquor establishments were "joints." New York was called simply "York"; Chicago was "Chi"; Boston, "Bean Town."

Criminals generally agreed, Flynt reported, that "Chi" was, from their viewpoint, an "honest" town. By "honest" they meant something different from what the average citizen meant. "Chi," they said, was "honest" in its dishonesty; a contract was a contract, and police would not go back on it. "York" was not so reliable. It was hypocritical. Police might give "the guns" clearance for a racket; but then, if reformers howled, they would turn around and clamp down on the very criminals whose money they had taken.

It was the professional opinion of criminals who knew cities from coast to coast that "Chi" was "the best stopping place for tramps and thieves in the United States." Flynt illustrated the virtues of "Chi" by citing the expert opinion of one, Wyoming Slivers. Slivers, he wrote, didn't care if Flynt used his name because it was so well known to the police anyway. Slivers was unusual, a kind of gentlemanly tramp with an engaging manner, a front that had enabled him some years previously to marry a well-to-do widow in Minnesota. Flynt reported:

"When she died she left him $10,000 to do as he liked with, and he elected to invest it in a six-months spree in which all of Hoboland was invited to take part. Slivers came out of the adventure minus three fingers and an ear, but before it was over ten of his pals lay down and died in different parts of the West."

Wyoming Slivers, when Flynt saw him, was well-dressed for a tramp and seemed to have some money. He spoke of "Chi" in these glowing terms:

"I like it 'cause it's honest. The City Hall gang went into

office on the promise that the town was to be open, an'
they've kept it open. Course they've got to put on a little
bluff when the reformers get after 'em, but I know, an'
the push knows, that Chi is goin' to be 'right' for the likes
o' you and me as long as the gang is in power."

By conservative estimate, Flynt reported, there were
50,000 thieves and tramps in Chicago at the time. He added:
"It is the opinion of the known 'grafters' that the big 'steals'
in Chicago are perpetrated by men who are officially recognized as respectable members of the community, and the
council was spoken of as an exceptionally well-trained 'stall'
to assist in picking the public's pocket. An old bank burglar
with whom I talked went so far as to say that one of the
councilmen used to be a saloonkeeper, in whose care he
(the bank burglar) and his pals left their burglar tools
between 'jobs.'"

In "York," Flynt interviewed one of the city's top law-
enforcement officials, a man known in the underworld as
"an ex-gun." Flynt added: "His photo as a known thief
may still be seen in Chicago. He is generally to be found
about 11 o'clock at night in the up-town haunts, where he
'rubbers' around, makes a 'pinch' occasionally, keeps track
of new-comers in the haunts, and takes as much 'scale'
as his position allows."

New York, so recently shaken by the Lexow probe, posed
as a "closed berg," Flynt wrote—but it was not. "No one
smiles more broadly than the gun," he reported, "when
one of the Powers that Rule goes before a grand jury or
an Assembly Investigating Committee and says that he
has no personal knowledge of certain 'joints'; and no one
is better informed than the gun of how much the Front
Office could tell if it wanted to."

The wave of reform and the excitement about "corrupt policemen, gambling dens, and disorderly houses" would pass, the thieves thought, "and the town will then settle back into its customary indifference to such matters." Already, there was one spot, one of the most public in the city, where the mobs congregated and preyed on the average citizen. This was the famous Brooklyn Bridge, connecting the Lower East Side of Manhattan with Brooklyn across the East River. "'Mobs' of 'dips' can be found there practically every day," Flynt wrote, "and some of them are so grasping that they even 'snitch' the gold spectacles of old men and women" walking across the bridge. This could have been very easily stopped if the police had wanted to stop it, Flynt declared. He added: "The leader of one of the 'mobs' is a notorious thief who must surely be known to every 'wise' operative at police headquarters, and one of his 'side-partners' is a man who was let loose from Sing Sing not long ago."

So much for a New York reform that had not reformed. Flynt went on to Boston. He found that "Bean Town" also believed it had cleaned itself up. It had gone through a great, reforming purge in 1894, and proper Bostonians believed that vice had received such a setback it would never recover. On the surface, Flynt reported, Boston seemed cleaner, but after "a week or two in the South End and the West End," he found that not so very much had changed. There were disorderly houses in abundance, and there were any number of "speakeasies" or "clubs" that sold liquor long after the permitted hour. "The thieves do not seem to me to be so numerous as formerly," Flynt wrote. "The women of the street, on the other hand, constitute one of the largest armies of the kind that I can recall having seen in a city of 600,000 inhabitants . . . The Under World is so impressed with Boston as a 'hangout' of the people in question that it frequently refers to it as 'The Town of Women.'"

In any time and place, such disclosures, stripping the mask from the face of righteousness and pretense, could have been guaranteed to create an uproar. But in staid 1901 the shock was like that of some tremendous earthquake shaking the land. Stunned readers could hardly believe that the best and the worst were partners in crime and corruption, but Flynt's factual, down-to-earth recital carried with it a conviction that could not be denied. The explosive impact of *The World of Graft* made Flynt nationally famous. He was read by almost everyone. Concerned citizens, reformers, civic leaders simply had to read his book. And the police, of course, were furious. The head of the New York City detective division told reporters he was out to "get" Flynt, and he threatened to subject the little writer to what *McClure's* called "the Infamous Third Degree" if he were ever caught.

Flynt, however, had vanished. He never stayed long in one place anyway, and he kept well away from New York until a strong, reform district attorney had taken office and had given police more serious matters to worry about.

With the publication in 1901 of *The World of Graft*, Flynt's work was practically finished. Drink and cocaine were taking their toll of him. Though he was still young, only in his thirties, his physical and mental powers were failing. He still wrote. He did other exposés. But the fire, the zest were gone. Nothing that he wrote had the power or made the impact of *The World of Graft*.

That book had preceded the birth of the muckraking

era by a full year; but though Flynt lived until 1907, though he struggled to write during those first exciting years that saw muckraking at its whitest heat, he was not a part of the movement he had helped to create. He had pioneered. He had reported the raw stuff of life. He had shown the way for the man who was to become known as the first—and, perhaps, the greatest—of all the muckrakers.

CHAPTER IV

Lincoln Steffens

LINCOLN STEFFENS is generally credited with being the first muckraker, and he became in the public eye the muckraker of all muckrakers.

In appearance and personality, he was the very opposite of the kind of man one might expect. Here was no brash, six-foot, rough, tough reporter. On the contrary, Steffens was small and slim. He had large, intelligent eyes, a bushy mustache, a sharp-pointed little goatee, and he habitually wore narrow, string ties. The effect he created was that of a man who was alert, sharp, keen.

His manner, like his appearance, was the reverse of what might be expected of a man who exposed corruption in high places and low. Steffens was highly educated, mild-mannered, gently quizzical. He questioned much in the manner of Socrates, disturbing the self-satisfied by his ques-

39

tions since the questions themselves seemed to require surprising answers. In a word, Steffens was the gentleman muckraker—and, perhaps, all the more effective as a result. His urbane, polished manner seemed to invite confidences from all kinds of persons; he made it clear that he was not questioning to condemn, but only to find out. His attitude seemed to reassure even the hardest rogues; they got the feeling that he had no personal interest in blaming or pillorying them for whatever they might have done but that he was looking beyond them to issues larger than themselves.

Steffens was born in San Francisco in 1866, the son of Joseph and Elizabeth Steffens. His father, a wealthy merchant, soon moved with his family to Sacramento, where they lived in a three-story gingerbread castle crowned by a tower rising in the center above the entrance hall. This mansion at 16th and H Streets was purchased by the state in 1902 and became the official residence of the governors of California.

Sacramento in the 1870s, when Steffens was a boy, was a roaring river port. It was a center for miners, ranchers, shippers, and gamblers; it was also the state capital and so the scene of much of the skulduggery and corruption with which the period was rife. This atmosphere became part of the life of the growing boy. His parents had bought him a pony, and he roamed the countryside, meeting the rough characters of the region, aware of crudity and corruption.

His keen mind, however, set him apart from others. He was educated first in the public schools of Sacramento. Next he attended military academy in San Mateo and the University of California in Berkeley. Having absorbed as much as American education had to give him, he went off to Europe, and there for three years he studied in German universities, in the Sorbonne in Paris and also, later in London. He had been interested at first in history, philosophy, and science. His interest in art and ethics deepened as he studied; and when he thought of his future, he imagined himself as a philosopher or an artist or a novelist. There was always to be an artistic streak in him.

In the autumn of 1892, newly married, he returned to the United States, a young man adrift in his sea of education, not knowing exactly where he was headed but resigned to entering on a business career if that was what must be. It was therefore one of the shocks of his life when, as his ship reached quarantine in New York Harbor, he was handed a letter from his father. It read:

"My dear son, when you finished school you wanted to go to college. I sent you to Berkeley. When you got through there, you did not care to go into my business, so I sold out. You preferred to continue your studies in Berlin. I let you. After Berlin it was Heidelberg: after that Leipzig. And after the German universities you wanted to study at the French universities in Paris. I consented, and after a year with the French, you had to have a half year of the British Museum in London. All right. You had that too. By now you must know about all there is to know about the theory of life, but there's a practical side as well. It's worth knowing. I suggest that you learn it, and the way to study it, I think, is to stay in New York and hustle. Enclosed please find one hundred dollars, which should keep you until you can find a job and support yourself."

Steffens, who hadn't supported himself for a day in his life, had to sink or swim. Fortunately, he swam. Taking stock of himself, he decided that, since he wanted to write, he should become a reporter. He hounded newspaper offices until he got a job on the *Evening Post*, and soon he was on his way. He had a flair for writing, and his quick, curious mind made him an ideal journalist.

In seven years of furious work, he rose to the top of his profession. Those were days when New York seethed with reforming fervor. The Reverend Dr. Charles H. Parkhurst, posing as a sport of the times, frequented the wide-open gambling dens and houses of ill-fame, collecting evidence on wholesale police corruption. His findings so shocked the city that the state Lexow investigation followed and reform rode high.

Steffens reveled in the stuff of headlines. He roamed the city, talking to persons of both little and high importance. To all, he offered sympathetic understanding, and under his gentle questioning, many opened up. Both reformers and their targets trusted him. He talked equally with the Reverend Dr. Parkhurst and "Clubber" Williams, the police captain who was one of Parkhurst's targets. He interviewed J. P. Morgan, the colossus of Wall Street, and Richard Croker, the Tammany boss; and he decided that Croker was no more corrupt than many far more powerful and respectable figures in the city's business and social life—men who looked down their superior noses at the political manipulator whom they didn't hesitate to use for their own purposes.

Through it all, Steffens kept a certain perspective. He did not have much patience with holier-than-thou reformers. He considered many no better than the men they were attacking—and some not as good. But he respected reformers who were sincere and practical—men like Parkhurst; Jacob A. Riis, a fellow journalist who had exposed hideous slum conditions and was laboring to correct them; and Theodore Roosevelt as a furiously active, reform police commissioner.

In 1897 Steffens and a band of fellow journalists left the *Evening Post* and got control of the broken-down *Commercial Advertiser*. Steffens became city editor and assembled a highly capable and unusual staff. He sought out men who were more than just good reporters—men who could not only get the news but who had the intelligence and education to write it with style and grace. Ever a writer himself, he spruced up much of the copy by rewriting it with his own individualistic touch.

Steffens not only drove himself hard night and day at the *Advertiser;* he also wrote a number of magazine articles and stories, selling some of them to *McClure's.* He was also working on a novel, based on the career of one of the corrupt police captains whom he had come to know during the Lexow probe, and he had a contract to write a biography of Theodore Roosevelt, a project that he started but never completed because neither he nor Roosevelt could spare enough time for it in their ceaselessly active lives.

This was the situation when, in the spring of 1901, S. S. McClure offered Steffens the job of managing editor of *McClure's Magazine.* Steffens at first disliked the idea, but he had worked himself to the point of exhaustion and was faced with the danger of a nervous breakdown. His doctor warned him that he could not keep up the pace he had been setting, and he discovered that his associates on the *Advertiser* felt he was "'all in,' exhausted, 'used up.'"

In the end, therefore, he accepted McClure's offer, took three months to rest at a cabin on a lake in the Adirondacks, and then reported to *McClure's*, fit and eager for a new career.

It soon became apparent to McClure, however, that he had hired a man who was an excellent writer, but no editor. Steffens's best work for the magazine was done when he wrote articles for it himself or when he took someone else's lackluster work and whipped it into shape. Finally, McClure took Steffens aside and told him that, though he had been a newspaper editor, he was no magazine editor— and he would have to learn to be one.

"How can I learn?" Steffens asked, hurt and angry.

"Not here," McClure said. "You can't learn to edit a magazine here in this office."

"Where then can I learn?" Steffens asked. "Where shall I go to learn to be an editor?"

McClure sprang up and waved his arms in a circle.

"Anywhere," he said. "Anywhere else. Get out of here, travel, go—somewhere. Go out in the advertising department. Ask them where they have transportation credit. Buy a railroad ticket, get on a train, and there, where it lands you, there you will learn to edit a magazine."

Steffens found that the Lackawanna Railroad owed the magazine for advertising, and he ordered a ticket for Chicago. In this fashion, crazy as it may seem, the great muckraking era was about to be born.

Dumped down in Chicago, Steffens began to search for magazine material. A lawyer to whom he was introduced suggested that he go up to St. Paul, Minnesota, where "there's a very quiet little old German gentleman named Weyerhauser" who owned a huge amount of the nation's timberlands. "He's one of the richest men in America, richer than some of your famous New York millionaires, and the public has never heard of him," Steffens's informant said.

The tip sounded good, and Steffens went to St. Paul. He learned that Weyerhauser came to his office every morning at 7:30. Steffens made it a point to get there before him and lie in wait. When Weyerhauser came in, Steffens asked him for an interview. "I am never interviewed," Weyerhauser said. "I don't care for write-ups."

He was brushing past into his office when Steffens stopped him by saying: "I don't propose to write you up. I propose to write you down."

Weyerhauser whirled, looked, and evidently decided that this was a different kind of reporter. He invited Steffens into his office, and there Steffens told him he understood Weyerhauser had started with nothing and had acquired a fortune and "half the forests of America." Then he asked: "What did it cost you?"

Weyerhauser stared, started to shake his head in denial; but then he got Steffens's meaning, and his face became serious. "You mean—" he said.

"Yes, I mean that there are lots of able men in this country who have set out with no capital, made millions, and then tell us it cost them nothing but work, hard work. I think it cost them—something else. I think it cost them as much or more than they made. How rich are you?"

This was the student of ethics speaking, and the questions pierced the hard shell Weyerhauser had erected around himself. All morning the millionaire lumberman and the reporter talked; all morning, Weyerhauser unburdened himself. He was a deeply disturbed man; he had been longing to pour out his feelings of guilt to someone. He described the deals, the political payoffs, the corrupt bargains that he had had to make "to do business"—and to keep on doing more and more business. He was a man on a treadmill, driven on and on no matter how many millions he accumulated, consumed by the demands of the ever-swelling business monster he had himself created. The details would have created a sensation, but there was just one hitch. Before Weyerhauser poured out his soul to Steffens, he extracted a promise that everything he said would be treated in confidence; and so Steffens, bound by his pledge of secrecy, returned to Chicago without a story.

There his lawyer friend had another idea. Down in St. Louis, he said, there was a prosecutor, Joseph Wingate Folk, who was raising a storm about the bribery of the board of aldermen, the city's governing body. "We get the dust of it in the papers here, but no clear idea of what it's all about," Steffens's friend said.

The idea appealed to Steffens at once. He had been thinking that magazines could fill a special, important function. Across the nation, in various localities, headline stories developed from day to day. The details were fragmented, spread out over days and weeks in the local press until their full meaning became lost to the reader. Steffens theorized that a magazine could take such developments and pull all the details together in a single article that would make sense and have impact. Folk's reform crusade in St. Louis struck him as just the kind of vehicle he needed to test the theory.

Steffens hurried off to St. Louis, and by noon of the following day he was sitting with Folk in a quiet corner of the Planters Hotel lobby. Folk was a short, small-boned man, with thin black hair and dark eyes. He was an innocent who had blundered, all unsuspecting, into a sink of corruption; and he was dazed, hardly able to believe that things were as bad as all the evidence showed him they were.

Folk—it was almost laughable—was one of those accidents of politics that sometimes do in the politicians. He had come to St. Louis from Tennessee and started a career as a corporation attorney. He had dabbled a bit in politics to gain practice in public speaking and to make friends and win clients. He had had no interest in the criminal law, and it was entirely by accident—indeed, against his own wishes—that he had become a prosecutor. It so happened that the political bosses had been squabbling among themselves at the time; they had been unable to agree on a candidate for circuit attorney, as the prosecutor's post was called; and so they had reached a compromise. They had settled on apparently harmless, obliging Joe Folk, a man who wouldn't cause anybody any trouble. Ed Butler, the city's big Democratic boss, had informed the reluctant Folk that he had been literally drafted for the prosecutor's post.

"I'll have to do my duty," Folk had warned him.

"Oh, sure," said Butler, the worldly wise political boss who expected a candidate to say just that—but never expected a candidate to mean it.

The difficulty was Joe Folk meant it. Talking to Steffens, Folk was still in a state of shock as he described how Butler had walked into his office after the election and had started issuing orders. "Joe, you will name So-and-So your first assistant, this and that man the second and third, and—

47

you will let our ballot-stuffers go and give the other bosses' repeaters the limit—"

Recalling the scene, Folk told Steffens his reaction:

"I and my office, the criminal law, was to be run by—criminals!"

Folk had balked. He had started prosecuting men who had gone around stuffing ballot boxes. It had been the turn of "Boss" Ed Butler to be shocked. "But they elected you, Joe," he had told the young prosecutor. "Without them and us you wouldn't be where you are."

"I am doing my sworn duty," answered upright Joe Folk.

"Well, then, we'll get you," Butler threatened.

"Not until I've first got you," Folk told him.

That had been just the beginning. The political bosses had caught a tartar. Mild-mannered, little Joe Folk was a rarity in their experience. He was a man who really believed in all the ideals of honesty and decency and fair play about which politicians only orated; and he was that double-rarity, a man with a stiff backbone. They couldn't bribe, pressure, or threaten him with any success, no matter what it cost him personally.

Once Folk started out on the trail of corruption, it wasn't long before he stumbled into a veritable cesspool. The Suburban Railway Company had been granted a franchise to run its lines along St. Louis's streets. Folk heard rumors that it had obtained its franchise through the wholesale bribery of public officials. He subpoenaed nearly one hundred of the most prominent citizens of St. Louis before a grand jury—councilmen and other local officials, officers and directors of Suburban Railway, bank presidents and cashiers. The outcry rocked the heavens, and again Folk was shocked—this time by "the prominence and respectability of the men and women who intercede for crooks."

These pleas, wailings, threats only made Folk a more determined little bulldog. He hammered away until some of those on the inside of the deal, thinking he knew more than he actually did, broke and confessed everything. They named names, prices, dates when the money was passed; they told exactly who got what and who paid whom.

Still stunned by his momentous, eye-opening discoveries, Folk summed up for Steffens:

"It is good businessmen that are corrupting our bad politicians; it is good business that causes bad government— in St. Louis."

He described how all the confessing bribe-givers and bribe-takers had told him: "That's the way it's done, Mr. Folk; you can't do business any other way."

And Folk expressed his shock at all this by exclaiming: "Bribery is no mere felony. It's treason."

This was a conclusion that the muckrakers themselves were to reach again and again before they were finished.

Steffens had the sensational story he had been seeking, but he still thought of himself as an editor, not a reporter, and so he hunted for someone else to write it. Folk suggested a St. Louis reporter named Claude H. Wetmore; Steffens saw Wetmore, told him *McClure's* wanted an article on Folk and the corruption of St. Louis. Then Steffens went back to New York.

When Wetmore's article came in, it wasn't at all what Steffens wanted. Wetmore had "gone easy" on the role played by the powerful Ed Butler; he had toned down some of the damning facts. When Steffens protested, Wetmore protested right back: he could not go on working

49

and living in St. Louis if he wrote the whole truth and nothing but the truth.

Steffens insisted that the article had to be stronger, and he wrote into it some of the things Folk had told him. Wetmore said that, if this was the way it was to be, Steffens's name would have to be on the article, too, so that he could shift the blame. Steffens agreed. And so the article under their two by-lines appeared in the October 1902 issue of *McClure's*.

It was entitled "Tweed Days in St. Louis"—a title that implied St. Louis was operating under the same kind of corrupt system that had prevailed in New York during the days of Boss Tweed—and it suggested that what was happening in St. Louis was not unique, but that it was typical of a pattern of corruption existing in cities throughout the land. Readers were shocked. The article created a sensation, and it is generally credited with being the opening salvo in the barrage of muckraking that was soon to sweep the nation.

A look at some of the disclosures made in "Tweed Days in St. Louis" shows why it created the stir that it did. "The corruption of St. Louis came from the top," Steffens wrote. Originally, he said, "the best citizens—the merchants and financiers—" had been sincerely concerned for the welfare of the city, but about 1890 things changed—"public franchises and privileges were sought, not only for legitimate profit and common convenience, but for loot." And once the looting began, there was no stopping it; every vote carried its price tag.

The St. Louis governing body was divided into two houses, an upper Council and a lower House of Delegates. Saloon-keepers infested both bodies. One of Folk's grand juries declared it found a number of these municipal fathers "utterly illiterate and lacking in ordinary intelligence . . . In some, no trace of mentality or morality could be found . . ."

Under such rulers, bribery became systematized. Steffens wrote: "There was a price for a grain elevator, a price for a short switch; side tracks were charged for by the linear foot . . . ; a street improvement cost so much; wharf space was classified and precisely rated. As there was a scale for favorable legislation, so there was one for defeating bills. It made a difference in the price if there was opposition, and it made a difference whether the privilege asked was legitimate or not. But nothing was passed free of charge . . ."

Steffens became even more specific. He continued: "A member of the House of Delegates admitted to the grand jury that his dividends from the [bribery] combine netted $25,000 in one year; a councilman stated that he was paid $50,000 for his vote on a single issue."

And those were days, it must be remembered, when the dollar was worth some ten times what it is today.

It is little wonder, then, that Steffens's first exposé created a tempest. Was this the way things *really* were? Were other cities, as Steffens implied, equally corrupted? Was corruption itself a way of life, a way of government? Steffens was convinced that the answer to all these questions was "yes"; and, with McClure's backing, he set out to document the case.

His experience in St. Louis had convinced him of one thing: he would have to get the facts and write the articles himself. The kind of true, no-punches-pulled exposés he envisioned could not be obtained from local reporters, subject to the home-town pressures that had daunted Wetmore.

But where should Steffens go next? The choice was obvious. The press of the nation had been reporting sketchy details about a major police scandal in Minneapolis, the great city of the northern Midwest. Steffens would go there, pull all the details together and put the scandal into focus. "We'll call it 'The Shame of Minneapolis,'" McClure declared happily before Steffens left.

The publisher's anticipations were justified. In Minneapolis, Steffens uncovered another horror story. The graft in Minneapolis, he found, had been in the hands of the city's boss mayor, Dr. A. A. Ames, and the mayor's brother, Colonel Fred W. Ames, who had been made police chief. The police and criminals had been partners in loot. There had been a payoff scale for everything—for houses of prostitution, gambling dens, illegal liquor joints. Since the city officials and the crooks had been in partnership, the gambling games were rigged, the wheels fixed, the players played for suckers, fleeced and then driven out of town. There was even worse, Steffens wrote. "Confidence men, porch climbers, burglars and all sorts of thieves were not only permitted to operate, with the police to watch them work, to protect them from interruption and prevent them from holding out on the mayor and his cabinet; word was also passed out to the underworld outside that clever crooks would be welcomed in Minneapolis if they would play fair with the police . . ."

The result: "Burglaries were common, many of them planned by the police. One case established on the court records was the robbery of the Pabst Brewing Company office. The officers persuaded an employee to learn the combination of the safe, and, with a regular burglar, to clean it out one night, while the police captain and the detectives stood guard outside."

What impressed Steffens, what was always to impress him, was not the deed so much as the evidence of an established pattern. This was the way the American system was working, not just in Minneapolis, but in cities throughout the land. "The police graft system of Minneapolis," he later wrote, "was like the police graft system of its so-called Twin City, St. Paul, across the river. It was the same as in Seattle, Portland, San Francisco, Chicago, New Orleans, and of most of the cities in between."

The lid had been lifted off the steaming pot in Minneapolis by a courageous grand jury foreman, Hovey C. Clarke. Clarke had driven Mayor Ames and his corrupt administration out of the city, and his grand jury had indicted both the policemen and their underworld partners. Clarke had an ace in the hole in a couple of "big mitt men" (the underworld slang for a slick poker dealer who could "mitt" the right cards), and these two, feeling they had been double-crossed by their official partners, had turned over to Clarke "a small butcher book, a rough, well-kept ledger of stealings and divisions week by week." Steffens was eager to talk to the two "mitt men," Billy Edwards and Charlie Howard; and he finally persuaded Clarke to tell him where they were hidden. He also obtained the loan of the Big Mitt Ledger, saying he wanted the pair to explain some of the entries.

Thus equipped, Steffens visited Edwards and Howard. He soon had the pair talking, not just about the ledger, but about crime across the nation. The system was the same everywhere, they told him. They had been working on the West Coast—Seattle, Portland, San Francisco, and Los

Angeles—when Minneapolis police, needing skilled hands for their crooked games, had issued a call for them to come and practice their arts. They had come, but their promised protection in Minneapolis had broken down. This was not because the city had had an outbreak of virtue, but because the corruption had become so bad, the bribe-takers had become so greedy, that one faction began to knock off the others' crooks. Feeling themselves greatly wronged, Edwards and Howard had "squealed" and turned over to Hovey Clarke the Big Mitt Ledger.

This was the surface story, but Steffens, as always, was not content to stop here. He probed deeply. Why had it happened? What elements in society had made such crime and corruption possible? In Minneapolis, he found the same answers he had found in St. Louis and that he was to find later in other cities; the so-called "best citizens" were the ones who had sold out their community for the sake of private greed.

Hovey Clarke's grand jury campaign had chased the rascals out and had brought to power a reform administration headed by Acting Mayor D. Percy Jones. Steffens went to see Jones, and he found that Jones was in deep trouble. The reform mayor had started out determined to enforce the law to the letter, but he had quickly found there was little he could do about prostitution. Minneapolis was the haven for Northwest lumberjacks who came to town roaring for a good time. And so the mayor and his new police chief decided to restrict the women of the street to a remote section of the city and let prostitution run—only now without payoffs, without corruption.

This compromise solution touched off a storm. Oddly enough, Mayor Jones discovered, the most angry were the "good citizens, property owners, whose houses were cleaned of prostitution" and who, as a consequence, "rose up in wrath against this arrangement, which lost them their high rent. More astonishing to the good mayor, these landlords were able to set the clergy and other good citizens after him for compromising with sin . . ."

Steffens's article on Minneapolis was published in the January 1903 issue of *McClure's,* accompanied by a reproduction of the first page of the Big Mitt Ledger. The article was an immediate sensation and made Steffens nationally famous. Newsstand sales quickly exhausted the issue of the magazine, subscriptions poured in, and the mail brought letters of praise and advice. From cities, towns and even villages, letter-writers urged: "Come here to this place; you will find scandals that will make Minneapolis and St. Louis look like models of good government."

S. S. McClure, canny publisher that he was, knew that he had tapped a vein of public interest. To keep that interest at fever heat—and, incidentally, to keep selling more and more magazines—he needed ever more sensational disclosures. This was a compulsion that was to help discredit muckraking in the end; but fortunately for McClure, he had in Steffens and others solid reporters who could produce sensations that were soundly researched and completely true.

With McClure eager for a new and even more startling exposé, there was much discussion among the magazine's editorial staff about what Steffens should do next. Steffens himself finally carried the day. He wanted to return to St. Louis. He wanted to learn how Folk was making out; he wanted to probe the St. Louis situation in greater depth.

55

It was a wise choice because, as he soon discovered, Folk was in deep trouble.

As it had been in Minneapolis, so was it in other cities Steffens was to investigate later, the "good" citizens of St. Louis were all for reform and honest government—up to a point. It turned out to be a very limited point. The instant reform began to hurt—to limit the profits "good" citizens made from slum dwellings, to deny some business concern in which they were interested a crooked deal that would have made it a bundle of money—at that point, at that instant, the "good" citizen turned against reform and clamored for the return to power of a corrupt political machine with which he could do the kind of business that would fatten his pocketbook.

Folk sensed the mood of the city he had been trying to purify and confessed to Steffens: "I am beaten already in St. Louis. I have to try Boss Butler in some other town; I couldn't convict him in St. Louis. The people are against me." He paused, added: "I can't be reelected here either . . . The voters of St. Louis will beat me and—what I stand for."

Steffens told Folk there was only one solution: he would have to carry his case to the people of Missouri; he would have to run for governor. "Of course," cried Folk enthusiastically, throwing down his napkin on the table at which they were dining. "But of course. All the boodle trails lead up to the State Legislature. I'll go there . . ."

The result of this suggestion was that Folk ran for governor of Missouri and was elected at a time when he could not have been reelected circuit attorney in St. Louis. Missouri voters were for reform and purity in government, at least technically, but the time would come when they too, would tire of the kind of government that barred them from the crooked, but profitable, deal—and, when that time came, Folk, who had loomed as a possible candidate for President, would be finished politically.

All of that, of course, was in the future. As for the present, events quickly demonstrated for Steffens that Folk's assessment of the reaction of the "good" citizens of St. Louis was correct in every detail. The spunky prosecutor got Boss Butler's trial shifted to Columbia, a university town, and there he persuaded a jury to convict the boodling boss. Folk's tactic at the trial was simple, admirable, effective. He did not attack Butler personally; he held him as a symbol. Democracy itself was on trial, he said; Missouri was on trial if it sanctioned the corruption of Butler and his gang. The "good" citizens of Missouri who sat on the jury panel bought the argument, and it seemed for the moment that justice had triumphed.

But Steffens found that, back in St. Louis, the "good" citizens of boodle town were not buying the verdict at all. Everywhere he heard the prediction that "Butler would never wear pin stripes." It was a prophecy that was fulfilled in startling fashion. Steffens later wrote in his *Autobiography*:

". . . The boss himself behaved wisely. He stayed indoors for a few weeks—till a committee of citizens from the best residence section called upon him to come out and put through the House of Delegates a bill for the improvement of a street in their neighborhood. And Butler had this done. One of the first greetings to Folk was a warning from a high source that now he had gone far enough. He paid no heed to this. He proceeded to the trial of other cases. One of them was of Henry Nicolaus, a rich brewer, for bribery. Mr. Nicolaus pleaded that he did not know what was to be the use of a note for $140,000 which he had endorsed. Pretty bad? The judge immediately took the case from the jury and directed a verdict of not guilty. This was the first case Folk had lost; he won the next eight, making his record fourteen won to one lost. But the Supreme Court took up the fight. Slowly, one by one, then wholesale, this highest court of appeal reversed the boodle cases. The machinery of justice broke down under the strain of boodle pull. And the political machinery did not break down. The bi-partisan gang, with reformers and businessmen for backers, united on a boodle ticket, elected it, and—Boss Butler reorganized the 'new' House of Delegates with his man for speaker and the superintendent of his garbage plant (in the interest of which he offered the bribe for which he was convicted) for chairman of the Sanitary Committee!"

Steffens went to other cities and found the same conditions. Pittsburgh was bad; Philadelphia, worse. In the City of Brotherly Love, in fact, Steffens found a political machine so powerful, so entrenched, that it made New York's corrupt Tammany Hall chieftains look like amateurs—and left Philadelphians in complete despair of ever being able to do anything about it. A hotelman told Steffens how, when he went to vote, he was told he had "voted already." When he protested and threatened to kick up a terrible fuss, he was finally permitted to vote, "but they called in a couple of gangsters to offset my ballot by voting the other way—in the names of George Washington and Benjamin Franklin."

Steffens found that the Philadelphia machine had rammed through a whole series of franchise steals, one after another, brazenly advertising the wholesale thefts. Steffens was astounded. How could any political machine afford to flaunt its thievery so openly, without even the pretense of a coverup? He went to see the political boss, Israel W. Durham, and Durham, to his amazement, talked to him frankly, explaining everything.

"If we did any one of these things alone," Durham said, "the papers and the public would concentrate on it, get the facts, and fight. But we reasoned that if we poured them all out fast and furious, one, two, three—one after the other—the papers couldn't handle them all and the public would be stunned and—give up. Too much . . . We know that public despair is possible and that that is good politics."

Such experiences forced Steffens to some conclusions about the nature of the American political system, and he expressed his thoughts to Durham in these words:

"Political corruption is, then, a process. It is not a temporary evil, not an accidental wickedness, not a passing symptom of the youth of a people. It is a natural process by which a democracy is made gradually over into a plutocracy . . . If this process goes on, then this American republic of ours will be a government that represents the organized evils of a privileged class."

Durham listened, and Steffens soon discovered that the political boss was a man of imagination, capable of grasping all the implications Steffens was finding in the system. Oddly enough, Durham formed a habit of visiting Steffens in his hotel room and discussing with him the philosophy of politics—and corruption. It was a strange friendship, that of the political boss and the muckraker who had come to expose him, but Durham was an unusual man.

He had grown up in the system and had adopted its

methods without questioning. He had been loyal to his party and his friends. He had played the game the way he had been taught it was to be played, and he had made deal after deal without appreciating what all the deals totaled. But, deep down, once Steffens started him thinking about the larger picture, he had the decency to be disturbed. Like Weyerhauser, the lumber tycoon, he began to question the basis on which he had operated all his life, and he began to regret that he was too old and ill to be able to change anything. "I have had many experiences since with big, bad men," Steffens later wrote, "and I find that, if they are big enough and bad enough, they seem to be as eager to do great good as great evil. They simply are not asked to do good; the drift of things, the rewards, the applause and education, are all the other way."

In 1904, Steffens collected the articles he had written for *McClure's* and published them in book form under the title *The Shame of the Cities*. The volume became a handbook on American city government; it was then, and it remains today, one of the clearest explanations ever written of how the American system works at the basic local level. In an introduction, Steffens explained that he was not blaming any one class for the evils that he had found. This was true. His researches showed that virtually all classes wanted special favors from government—and were willing to pay bribes to get them. Big business drew a heavy share of the blame simply because it was big and powerful—and, therefore, had more clout. It was big business that had undermined a ten-year reform administration in Chicago, but it was not big business alone that had cast out a reform administration in New York and returned Tammany

Hall to power. That deed had been performed because New Yorkers generally had become disenchanted with the price they had to pay for clean government; even historic Trinity Church, located on Broadway opposite the mouth of Wall Street, hadn't liked reform. Why? Because Trinity owned and made a huge profit from some of the worst slums in the city—and wanted nothing to interfere with its take. The greed of all classes for special privileges, for special dispensations, was the underlying factor in the wholesale corruption of American city governments. "The misgovernment of the American people is misgovernment by the American people," Steffens proclaimed.

But if this was true of the cities, what about the states? Did the system end with city government or did it operate in the same fashion at the state and national levels? Steffens had seen enough in Missouri to believe that the same system functioned across the board in American politics, and so he started another series in *McClure's* on the shame of the states. He went first to Missouri, where Folk had been elected governor, and he reported his findings in an article entitled "Folk's Fight for Missouri." It was, Steffens wrote years later in his *Autobiography*, his most effective political exposé—the one article in which he brought all the pieces together. He summed it up this way:

"In brief it showed that the business corruption of politics and government in Missouri was the same as in the city of St. Louis—the same methods, the same motives, purposes, and men, all to the same end: to make the state officials, the Legislature, the courts, part of a system representing the special interests of bribers, corruptionists, and criminals; that acts of bribery and corruption done as a

61

series of felonies form a continuous process which trans-
forms the theoretically democratic government of the state
and its cities into a plutocratic system which deserves the
people and serves the seekers of privileges."

In Missouri, Steffens also discovered that bribery was a
flourishing interstate business. Railroads, powerful business
trusts, public service corporations, schoolbook publishers,
even a baking-powder company—all had interests that
stretched well beyond the borders of a single state; all
operated everywhere on the theory that you paid what you
had to pay for the favors that favored your business. The
interstate lobbyist for the national baking-powder trust told
Steffens that his millionaire boss and himself "had been
active in twenty-four states, which they found . . . all
ripe and ready for them, so corrupted by their own business
men that a national visitor with money was more than
welcome."

As always, Steffens found powerful men among the bribers
and corruptionists who had come to recognize the enormity
of their guilt through his exposés. A man whom he identified
only as "the chief attorney for the big boodlers" privately
supplied him with some court records that he needed and
told him: "You are right. We are wrong; I never realized
how wrong we were. You understand, we only thought we
were after this law or that franchise. We never stopped to
think that other men also wanted this or that, and that
all of us together were doing something rotten. We never
saw it whole the way you see it. It's fierce when you take
it all in at one gulp like this." And William Ziegler, the
powerful millionaire head of the baking-powder trust, read
Steffens's article with its unflattering references to himself,
laid it down several times to reflect, then finished it and

commented: "It's hell, isn't it? And I'm playing the very devil!"

Steffens's exposure of corruption on the state level caused widespread shock. This meant that corruption was not just a local matter, but it went up and up and infected the very highest governmental structures. Former President Grover Cleveland, who was then living in Princeton, New Jersey, was so disturbed by the implications that he asked Steffens to come and see him. Steffens went and found the bluff old man, who had begun his political career by exposing corruption in Buffalo, torn between contradictions: he recognized the truth of Steffens's report—but, at the same time, his mind boggled at accepting it.

"I have read that article, and I can't believe it," Cleveland said. "How can you believe all that with"—and he gestured out the window—"with the sun shining like that?"

He talked about democracy, about the American governmental system to which Steffens had held up such a revealing—and damning—mirror.

"I'm not doubting your report on Folk's evidence," he said. "It is the picture as a whole that I cannot accept. No, no, I don't doubt that either. It is true. I have seen it myself in office. I simply cannot make my imagination look at it as it is. It is too terrible. You will have to repeat and repeat that story, in other states, to get it through our heads."

Steffens went on to do just that, and he had a lot of help from his fellow muckrakers. As he had exposed the seamy side of politics, they exposed other equally tarnished aspects of American life. What Steffens had done to politics, an associate of his on *McClure's* did to business. This muckraker was the most unusual of them all—a quiet, self-possessed woman who looked more like a schoolmarm than a journalist. Yet she was the one who tackled the giant of giants, the great Standard Oil Company of John D. Rockefeller.

CHAPTER V

Ida M. Tarbell

ONE SPRING DAY in 1892, the energetic, mercurial S. S. McClure bounded up four flights of stairs to an apartment in Paris where a little-known American writer was living. The writer who received him was a tall woman with glossy black hair combed back from a wide brow and piled in a bun on top of her head. She had bright, intelligent eyes; a fine straight nose; firm lips above a strong but rounded chin. She habitually wore severe, high-collared dresses, and these gave her the prim air of a schoolmarm. The overall impression she created was one of calmness, coolness, detachment.

Back in New York before leaving on one of his regular talent-scouting trips to Europe, McClure had noticed an article on his editor's desk—"The Paving of the Streets of Paris" by M. Alphand. It had been written by Ida M.

Tarbell. McClure had read the article and had been impressed by its style; and so later, finding himself in London with time on his hands, he had decided to hop over to Paris and look up Miss Tarbell.

Such was the sequence that brought together for the first time the most striking magazine publisher of his day and the woman who was to become the most unusual star among his star-studded staff. In Ida Tarbell's apartment that day in 1892 McClure bubbled over as he described his grandiose plans for the great magazine he envisioned—one that was then struggling merely to stay alive. Ida Tarbell listened with that cool detachment of hers, and she was not too much surprised when the fast-talking McClure borrowed $40 from her before he left.

"I'll never see that money again," she later recalled saying to herself.

In this she was wrong. Much to her surprise, the $40 was promptly repaid, and this was to be by no means the last she was to hear of S. S. McClure. Two years later, McClure hired her to join the staff of his magazine and paid her expenses for the voyage across the Atlantic to New York. Among all of McClure's many instinctive and successful moves, this has to be judged the most brilliant.

Ida Minerva Tarbell had been born in 1859 almost at the very time and spot that saw the first oil gusher brought in. Her home was less than thirty miles from Titusville, Pennsylvania, where that historic event occurred. Her parents, Esther and Frank Tarbell, were well-educated, industrious, middle-class Americans. The family enjoyed occasional trips to Cleveland and family picnics on Chautauqua Lake. Crusading suffragettes often visited their home;

and, listening to their impassioned talk about women's rights, Ida Tarbell, as a young girl, came to a firm resolution.

"I must be free," she told herself, "and to be free I must be a spinster."

At fourteen, she got down on her knees and prayed to God to save her from marriage.

She graduated from Titusville High School and entered Allegheny College at Meadville, Pennsylvania. She was the only girl in a freshman class of forty "hostile or indifferent" to boys, she later wrote. She had intended at first to become a biologist, but she soon turned to writing. At twenty-six she became the associate editor of *The Chautauquan,* then one of the foremost literary periodicals. She remained with the magazine until 1889, but she became increasingly restive at the confining chores of her editorial role.

Ida Tarbell wanted to write biographies, but as she looked about her at the American literary scene, biographical writing seemed to her to be in a crude and primitive state. So she decided to go to Paris to study. There she enrolled in the Sorbonne and the Collège de Paris, taking writing courses, practicing her art, writing some magazine articles to earn money—and it was there that S. S. McClure discovered her.

When Ida Tarbell joined the staff of McClure's struggling magazine, one of its competitors, the *Century,* was making quite a splurge with a life of Napoleon that had been in preparation for years. McClure decided to meet the competition by putting Miss Tarbell to work on *The Short Life of Napoleon Bonaparte.* She wrote it "on the gallop," as she later said, in just six weeks. McClure, who was way ahead of his time in the use of pictures, illustrated the series lavishly, the magazine's circulation rose, and the publisher and his editors began to think that they might soon be out of financial danger.

Having scored such a success with one biography, they decided to put Ida Tarbell to work on another. And what more likely subject could there be than America's own martyred Civil War President, Abraham Lincoln?

When word got around in literary circles that Ida Tarbell was working on a Lincoln biography, there was much scoffing. The *Century* for two years had been running installments of an impressive *Life* written by Nicolay and Hay, both of whom had served under Lincoln, had known him personally and had quantities of original material at their fingertips. But the Nicolay-Hay *Life* had worked no miracles for the *Century's* circulation, and so the announcement that another Lincoln biography was to appear in *McClure's* caused Richard Watson Gildern, *Century's* editor, much amusement. "I hear," he said scornfully, "that *McClure's* has a girl doing another book on Lincoln."

It was a day and age when "girls" simply were not writers—not, that is, unless they stayed home and wrote romantic fiction, an acceptable avocation. The idea that a mere "girl" could do a hard, tough job of research and cap it with vivid and masterful writing seemed utterly preposterous. But Ida Tarbell's *Early Life of Abraham Lincoln* shattered all prejudicial notions. This was not "a quickie" produced "at a gallop," but a careful, thorough job of research. Ida Tarbell went back to original sources in Kentucky, Indiana, and Illinois, and her painstaking digging turned up new facts and sidelights on the early life of Lincoln. McClure, just as he had with her *Napoleon*, illustrated her text profusely, publishing many striking Lincoln pictures for the first time. The result was amazing.

McClure's circulation, which had been only 120,000 in August 1895, soared by leaps and bounds. By December, it was 250,000 and still growing. Ida Tarbell's life of Lincoln, McClure himself later said, "told on our circulation as nothing ever had before"; and by 1900, on the eve of the muckraking age, *McClure's* was going into 350,000 homes and was second in circulation only to its bitter rival, *Munsey's*.

This phenomenal success convinced McClure that he had in Ida Tarbell a writing treasure, and he began to cast about for a new subject of sufficient magnitude for her talents. He recalled that, during the Chicago World's Fair of 1892 and 1893, he had sent out a writer who had produced an article on Armour & Company, the great meatpacking house. The tone had been that big business was good; it represented the full flowering of the American free-enterprise system; it had worked miracles and turned a largely undeveloped nation into a major power in less than thirty years.

Most Americans of the time believed this and were content to worship at the shrine of business. The technological explosion that had followed the Civil War seemed a marvel of accomplishment. No one was asking, as Lincoln Steffens later was to ask, "What was the cost?" In 1897, when McClure began to think about turning Ida Tarbell loose on a big business series, nothing was further from his mind than that question of cost. He was thinking, as he later wrote, of a laudatory series on "the greatest American business achievements."

As McClure and his editors discussed the project, they recognized that some rumblings of discontent were beginning to be heard in the land. "The feeling of the common people," McClure recalled, "had a sort of menace in it; they took a threatening attitude toward the Trusts, and without much knowledge."

McClure reasoned that the public should be better informed; he had a feeling that the American people would like to hear more about the true inner workings of big business. But he and his editors agreed that it would be boring to discuss trusts in general. Why not take one great company as a typical example? Examine it to its roots, show how it was created, how it grew, how it achieved dominance in its field. Once this decision was made, the selection of the target was almost automatic. The Standard Oil Company was the greatest trust of the time, and it was the creation of one remarkable titan of the new business class—John D. Rockefeller. "There is no question that he is the Napoleon among businessmen," McClure said, and there was no question that Standard Oil was the "Mother of Trusts." This, then, would be Ida Tarbell's next assignment.

Miss Tarbell had been away from the oil districts of Pennsylvania for years, but her childhood memories were filled with images of "oil derricks, oil tanks, pipe lines, refineries, oil exchanges." The discovery of oil had changed her father's life. Frank Tarbell had been one of the early, independent oil producers—and he had been one of those driven to the wall in the ten years of business strife during which Standard Oil had forged its monopoly of the oil business. His partner, ruined by Standard, had shot himself, leaving Frank Tarbell with heavy notes to pay. These obligations had forced him to mortgage their home, a desperate measure that to him had been "unsound and humiliating."

When Frank Tarbell now learned that his daughter was going to write a series of articles about Standard Oil, his own experiences with the trust's enormous power made him fearful for her sake. "Don't do it, Ida," he pleaded. "They will ruin the magazine." Similar warnings came from others. They spoke of the "all-seeing eye and the all-powerful reach" of Standard Oil. If *McClure's* persisted in trying to tell Standard's story, these friends predicted, "They'll get you in the end."

Ida Tarbell was not to be frightened or deterred. She had been given a job to do, and she intended to do it. Methodically, thoroughly, she began to search for every scrap of information about Standard Oil. She dug into the files of long-forgotten law suits. She pursued the record of a Congressional investigation that had been mysteriously suppressed—and finally located a few rare copies in private hands. She interviewed businessmen who knew Rockefeller and had had dealings with him. Many were reluctant to talk, knowing Rockefeller's power, but others responded to her firm, dignified manner, realizing they could trust her. One Cleveland millionaire received her with calculated rudeness, his hat on, his feet propped on his desk, his face buried in a newspaper. Pretending not to notice, she began asking her calm, quiet, penetrating questions; and, as she did so, his feet came down from the desk, his face came up from the newspaper, and the hat came off his head.

This relentless pursuit of facts led Ida Tarbell down a long, long trail. For an incredible five years, she hunted and interviewed before her first article appeared in *McClure's*. It says much for S. S. McClure, a publisher whose like does not exist today, that once he had given his gifted writers their assignments he also gave them complete freedom to work and write as they saw fit. They could take as long as was needed to do a thorough job; however long it took, McClure would pay their salaries and stand the expense. He was willing to invest thousands of dollars in a single project; all he asked was results—and these he got in full measure.

Standard Oil, of course, could not long remain in ignorance of the fact that a dogged woman reporter was hunting the skeletons in its closet. It reacted as great corporations customarily react. It sought a prestigious name to act as its emissary, and it came up with the foremost man in American letters—Mark Twain. Twain called on McClure and asked him what the magazine intended to publish.

"You will have to ask Miss Tarbell," McClure told him.

Understanding correctly that the writer was not to be reached through the writer's publisher—the standard pressure approach then and now—Mark Twain next inquired whether Miss Tarbell would be willing to get Standard's side of the story from Henry R. Rogers, one of the corporation's vice-presidents. McClure left the decision up to Ida, and she said certainly, she would be glad to talk to Rogers. Some of her friends thought she was making a big mistake. "You'll become their apologist before you get through," they warned. They underestimated the steel in Ida Tarbell.

She paid her first visit to Standard's headquarters at 26 Broadway in New York City in the early winter of 1902. She was led through a maze of corridors to a reception room facing an open courtyard. There, while she waited for Rogers, she noticed the indistinct figure of a man behind a window across the courtyard—a man who seemed to be peeping at her stealthily. Whenever she visited Standard's offices—and her visits were frequent—she was led to the same waiting room, and she always noticed behind the distant window the same shadowy figure. Could it be, she wondered, that the elusive John D. Rockefeller was spying quietly on Ida Tarbell?

Though she never met Rockefeller, Miss Tarbell, through Rogers, talked to many other officials of the company. At the outset, she and Rogers made "a bargain." She agreed to take up with him each case in the company's history as she came to it. He promised to give her documents, figures, explanations, justifications—"anything and everything which would enlarge my understanding and judgment." She, however, was to remain the sole judge of her material, and she was to have a free hand in writing it as she saw fit.

The result of this novel arrangement and of Ida Tarbell's years-long research was a blockbuster series of articles that cast Standard Oil in the role of big-business villain and stirred the conscience of the nation. When McClure began the project, he had expected it to produce perhaps a total of three articles; Ida Tarbell wrote nineteen. The first installment in her series—later published in book form as *The History of the Standard Oil Company*—appeared in *McClure's* in November 1902, just one month after Steffens had broken muckraking ground with his "Tweed Days in St. Louis."

She told her story in prose that sang and that was backed up with hard, concrete details there could be no denying. In her first article, she set the scene. Drawing on the memories of her own childhood and the mass of information she had gathered in her years of research, she described the gold rush atmosphere of Pennsylvania after the first gusher was brought in at Titusville in 1857. Thousands poured into the region and boom towns sprang up with names like Pit Hole, Oil City, Petroleum Center, and Rouseville. "On every rocky farm," Ida wrote, "in every poor settlement of the region, was some man whose ear was attuned to Fortune's call, and who had the daring and energy to risk everything he possessed in an oil lease."

As in the gold rush days of the West, saloons, brothels, and dance halls sprang up, catering to the drifting mob of fortune seekers. But there had been through all the madness, Ida pointed out, a more stable element among the population of this new industrial frontier—sober, middle-class citizens like her own father and mother who had founded schools and churches and had done their best to bring up their children in a proper environment. At the close of this first installment, she teased her readers with a hint of the drama to come. Of the independent oil producers who had gambled their all in a hazardous new industry, she wrote:

"Life ran swift and ruddy and joyous in these men. They were still young, most of them under forty, and they looked forward with all the eagerness of the young who have just learned their powers, to years of struggle and development . . . There was nothing too good for them, nothing they did not hope and dare. But suddenly, at the very heyday of this confidence, a big hand reached out from nobody knew where, to steal their conquest and throttle their future."

"The big hand" was, of course, the hand of John D. Rockefeller and Standard Oil.

Ida painted a vivid picture of Rockefeller, and it was one that conflicted starkly with the "Horatio Alger" myth of the times—with the image of the poor boy who worked hard, was honest and upright, and rose by sheer merit to marry the boss's daughter and live forever after in the lap of a deserved luxury. Generations of Americans, who were fed this pap from boyhood, were reared in the belief that any boy, no matter how poor, if he worked hard enough and lived by all the Christian virtues, could climb the ladder of success without leaving a single muddy footprint behind him. Ida Tarbell's Rockefeller dealt a mortal blow to this complacent faith; her Rockefeller was less like Horatio Alger—and more like Charles Dickens's Scrooge.

In her second installment in *McClure's,* Ida described the rise of the great oil baron. He had been poor, it was true, and he had worked hard—but there the Horatio Alger symbolism ended. From boyhood, he had been a string-saver and penny-pincher. When he was only thirteen, Ida wrote, he had discovered that he could save his pennies until they built into dollars; that he could then lend small amounts at 7 per cent interest and make more money than he was being paid for digging potatoes. "It was a good thing," the boy reasoned, "to let money be my slave."

This was the cornerstone of the Rockefeller philosophy, Ida told her readers; money was everything. Rockefeller kept meticulous accounts of every penny that came into his hands; he noted and examined every expenditure, intent on making certain that not a cent was wasted. During the Civil War, he chose not to join the ranks, but to sell produce to the Union Army. And by the time the war ended, he had accumulated sufficient capital at the age of twenty-three to embark upon the major business enterprise of his life.

With sure instinct, he saw the possibilities in oil. It

could light the homes and provide the power for the new industrial America. But the wild gamble of drilling for oil—and, as so often happened, winding up with a dry well—was not for Rockefeller. He sought the sure thing— in this case, the profit to be made from refining the oil that others drilled. And so he established his first refinery in Cleveland, close to the new Pennsylvania oil fields.

The refinery prospered. Rockefeller was shrewd, a hard driver, and he had this passionate hatred of waste in any form. Where other companies permitted the residuum from their refining processes to drain away into the ground, Rockefeller struggled to find ways to save every drop, to find some use for it, to sell it at a profit, however small. "It hurt him to see it unused," Ida wrote, "and no man had a heartier welcome from the president of the Standard Oil Company than he who would show him how to utilize any portion of his residuum."

Rockefeller's greatest joy in life—indeed, it seemed his only joy—came from devising some new method to shave costs or from driving a hard bargain. "He had the frugal man's hatred of waste and disorder, of middlemen and un- necessary manipulation, and he began a vigorous elimina- tion of these from his business," Ida wrote. ". . . Old iron found its way into the junk shop. He bought his oil di- rectly from the wells. He made his own barrels. He watched and saved and contrived. The ability with which he made the smallest bargain furnishes topics to Cleveland story- tellers today. Low-voiced, soft-footed, humble, knowing every point in every man's business, he never tired until he got his wares at the lowest possible figure. 'John always got the best of the bargain,' old men tell you in Cleveland today, and they wince though they laugh in telling it.

'Smooth,' 'a savvy fellow,' is their description of him. To drive a good bargain was the joy of his life. 'The only time I ever saw John Rockefeller enthusiastic,' a man told the writer once, 'was when a report came in from the Creek that his buyer had secured a cargo of oil at a figure much below the market price. He bounded from his chair with a shout of joy, danced up and down, hugged me, threw up his hat, acted so like a madman that I have never forgotten it.'"

This was the man who now set out to control the entire oil industry of America.

To understand the mechanics of the scheme by which he bludgeoned his way to power, one must understand the geography of the oil regions at that time. The first producing wells were brought in along small runs and creeks in western Pennsylvania—a region that became known as "the Creek." Since the area was isolated and sparsely settled, railroads originally did not run spurs into the region. Hence oil had to be transported to the nearest railhead and shipped to refineries in more distant cities. Cleveland was the closest major metropolis, one with excellent rail connections with the East and a cheap water shipping route (unfortunately, closed by ice in winter) through Lake Erie and the Erie Canal to New York. These advantages made it the western capital of the oil refining business.

The refiners, even the crudest and least efficient of them, reaped tremendous profits, and soon more than thirty refineries in Cleveland were doing a flourishing business. But, with profits, came competition and change. Rail lines pushed connecting spurs into the Pennsylvania oil regions, and refineries, some of them modern and efficient, began to spring up along "the Creek." These refineries had an obvious economic advantage. They were located virtually at the oil well sites; they could refine oil right there; they could eliminate the double cost in oil shipments. The shipping detour to Cleveland became unnecessary, and refined oil could be sent directly to Eastern customers. The Cleveland oil refining bonanza was threatened.

Rockefeller's response to the threat both to Cleveland and to his own business was simple: every competitor must be driven to the wall. The device by which he accomplished this was the railroad freight rebate.

The railroads had been bankrolled, it will be recalled, by the free gift of public lands larger than all of the New England States and New York. The excuse for bestowing upon them this royal fortune in real estate was that they were performing a public service—as, indeed, they were. To protect the public interest, however, their charters specified that they must treat all sections of the public equitably: freight rates must be the same for everyone. In practice, this fairplay standard proved not to be worth the paper it was written on. The railroad barons piled up such enormous personal fortunes that they dominated the government that had created them; they became the economic kings of the age. And they began to act like kings. They cut freight rates at will for favored customers, and those not so favored, who could not get the same cutbacks, were priced out of business.

Canny John D. Rockefeller set out to turn this situation to his own advantage; he employed all his wiles to make certain he became one of those especially favored. Just how he finagled his first special deal with the railroads has never been disclosed, but by 1868 or 1869 his competitors in Cleveland began to be aware that some mysterious influence was working to their detriment. They were doing as much business as ever; they felt that on the whole they bought crude oil at the wells as cheaply as Rockefeller— but he was forging ahead at a fantastic rate, and their own profits were declining. What was going on? How could this be? Some Cleveland refiners decided the answer must be that Rockefeller was getting cheaper transportation rates.

One highly efficient Cleveland competitor—Alexander, Scofield & Co.—confronted railroad agents directly with the charge. Ida wrote:

"'You are giving others better rates than you are giving us,' said Mr. Alexander, the representative of the firm. They did not deny it—they simply agreed to give him a rebate also . . . Mr. Alexander was to pay the open, or regular, rate on oil from the Oil Regions to Cleveland, which at that date was forty cents a barrel. At the end of each month he was to send to the railroad vouchers for the amount of oil shipped and paid for at forty cents and was to get back from the railroad, in money, fifteen cents on each barrel. This concession applied only to oil bought at the wells. He was never able to get a rebate on oil shipped eastward. When he complained to the railroads he was told that if he would ship as large quantities as the Standard Oil Company he could have as good a rate.'"

This initial, illegal rebate scheme by which Rockefeller had undercut his competition was merely the pilot model for a colossal operation by which Standard Oil would achieve a virtual monopoly of the nation's oil business. In 1870 Rockefeller took the second step when his agents concluded a special agreement with General J. H. Devereux, vice-president of the Lake Shore Railroad. The agreement gave them a rebate on all oil shipped to the East as well as on that brought from the wells to Cleveland. Standard guaranteed to ship at least sixty barrels a day; and, in return, it was granted a shipping rate to the East far below that given to any of its competitors.

"It was equivalent to renting a railroad for their own private use," Ida Tarbell wrote. "Every Cleveland refiner was put out of the race by the arrangement . . . Firms which had been making $10,000 and $20,000 a year found themselves making little or nothing . . ."

The ordinary businessman, profiting so handsomely by a secret deal, would have been satisfied to take his profits and laugh—but not John D. Rockefeller. He had visions of empire in his head. And in late 1871 he began to take steps to make that vision a reality.

The scheme that was to bring the oil regions almost to the point of open warfare was suggested first by "certain Pennsylvania refiners," Ida Tarbell wrote. The idea was as simple as it was ruthless. A huge combination of principal refiners would be formed; the combination, because it would be refining and shipping oil in tremendous quantities, could then use its economic power to get even more favored treatment from the railroads. Not only would it be given rebates on its own shipments of oil, but it could demand and get rebates (or drawbacks as they were called) on the shipments of competitors. What this last provision meant was that a portion of the moneys paid by competing refineries to ship their oil at higher prices would be funneled right back into the pockets of Standard. The competitors, in effect, would be cutting their own throats with their own money.

To make this throat-cutting plot work, an innocent front

was needed. Ida Tarbell wrote that "a certain estate then in litigation had a charter for sale which gave its owner the right to carry on any kind of business in any country and in any way." This sweeping charter had been issued by a corrupt Pennsylvania legislature in such secrecy that the author and sponsors of the bill could never be identified. But there it was—a reality, a paper license for business fraud in the hands of a thing called the Southern (usually written South) Improvement Company.

Rockefeller and his associates snapped up the charter and began to sign up converts to their rate-fixing scheme. They exacted from every person they approached a pledge of absolute secrecy. This was a business that was to be done in the shadow of night, preferably the deep black of midnight.

The railroads, faced with the demands of the new combine, yielded one by one. To do them justice, the rail lines had their own problems. Each had tried to obtain for itself the lion's share of shipments from the oil regions, and so the lines had indulged in a price-cutting war that left them little profit. Consequently, this new proposal was attractive to them. All ruinous, free-enterprise competition would be eliminated. They would be dealing with a monopoly that could guarantee them regular shipments at a given rate, and this clearly meant better profits.

With self-interest on both sides dictating agreement, a pact was made with these specific terms: the open freight rate for the shipment of oil from Cleveland to New York was $2.56 a barrel at the time. But the South Improvement Company would be given a kickback of $1.06 on every barrel it shipped. Not only that; it would also be given the same $1.06 kickback on every barrel its rivals had to ship

81

at the open, or uncut, rate. Not only that; South Improvement would be given "full waybills of all petroleum shipped over the roads . . . This, of course, gave them knowledge of just who was doing business outside their company—of how much business he was doing, and with whom he was doing it . . ." This meant that the railroads, in effect, would become the spies for South Improvement.

Members of the conspiracy later admitted to a Congressional committee how enormous were the financial rewards of this agreement. In a day when a million dollars was worth probably ten times what it is today, they had expected to reap $6,000,000 annually from the freight rakeoff alone. In addition, by establishing a monopoly, they could control and raise prices—and gouge American consumers to the tune of another $7,500,000 a year.

These were the stakes, and they were so huge that no independent stood a chance of bucking the South Improvement combination. Once the railroads were in the bag, the stage was set for the blackjacking of all stubborn oil competitors. Ida Tarbell described the manner in which Rockefeller himself went about this delicate task:

". . . There were at that time some twenty-six refineries in town [Cleveland]—some of them very large plants. All of them were feeling more or less the effects of the last three or four years of railroad discriminations in favor of the Standard Oil Company. To the owners of these refineries Mr. Rockefeller now went one by one, and explained the South Improvement Company. 'You see,' he told them, 'this scheme is bound to work. It means an absolute control by us of the oil business. There is no chance for anyone outside. But we are going to give everybody a chance to come in. You are to turn over your refinery to my appraisers, and I will give you Standard Oil stock or cash, as you prefer, for the value we put upon it. I advise you to take the stock. It will be for your good.' Certain refiners objected. They did not want to sell. They did want to keep and manage their business. Mr. Rockefeller was regretful, but firm. It was useless to resist, he told the hesitating; they would certainly be crushed if they did not accept his offer . . ."

What happened to one refiner who was compelled to let Rockefeller, as the purchaser, set his own price for the purchase was typical. The resisting firm was Hanna, Blassington & Co., headed by Robert Hanna, uncle of Mark Hanna, the multimillionaire Ohio businessman who was later to become the political godfather of President William McKinley. The Hanna company had been refining oil since July 1869; and, in a sworn statement Robert Hanna later made, he declared it had reaped a 60 per cent return on its capital investment the first year and that it had averaged 30 per cent a year after that. When Hanna protested against Standard Oil's force play, Rockefeller told him: "You can never make any more money in my judgment. You can't compete with Standard. We have all the large refineries now. If you refuse to sell, it will end in your being crushed."

Hanna carried his protest to the railroads. They explained to him the facts of life. They would give him the same deal Rockefeller had—if he could guarantee them the same volume of shipments that Standard Oil did. Obviously, he couldn't do this. And since he couldn't, he was finished. Hanna recognized the inevitable, and Ida Tarbell described the final act of the drama in these words:

". . . They [the officials of the Hanna company] say that

83

they were satisfied they could no longer get rates to and from Cleveland which would enable them to live, and 're-luctantly' sold out. It must have been reluctantly, for they had paid $75,000 for their works, and had made 30 per cent a year on an average on their investment, and the Standard appraiser allowed them $45,000. 'Truly and really less than one-half of what they were absolutely worth, with a fair and honest competition in the lines of transportation,' said Mr. Hanna, eight years later, in an affidavit."

Under this kind of bludgeoning, the entire oil refinery business of Cleveland was brought to heel in three months' time—and on Rockefeller terms that were generous to Rockefeller. "Of the twenty-six refineries, at least twenty-one sold out," Ida Tarbell wrote.

The first two stages of the great monopoly plot had now worked so smoothly that only the victims had felt the stiletto as it sank between their ribs. The rest of Cleveland, the nation itself, had no conception of what was happening, for the Rockefeller combine had acted in strict accord with his favorite motto—"Silence is golden."

It remained now, with the railroads in agreement and Cleveland competition crushed, only necessary to complete the third phase of the operation—to crush, to eliminate, the independent oil refiners in the Oil Creek region. Again the bludgeon was to be Standard's power with the railroads. Freight rates were to be doubled—and that, the Rockefeller interests calculated, ought to fix the Oil Creek competition. But this time they had reckoned without their opposition. This time it was not to be so easy. The Oil Creek independents were made of sterner stuff than the Cleveland refiners; something of the old frontier spirit lived in them, and they were aroused to fury as the distant "big hand" reached out to crush them. They fought, and by fighting they stirred up a storm that shook the nation and led to the first exposure of Rockefeller and his methods.

The oil regions had heard rumors of the great conspiracy. At first they had not been able to believe such a thing was possible. But on the morning of February 26, 1872, the rumors were confirmed with shattering impact. New rail schedules for transporting oil from the Creek were announced—and the tariffs were doubled. Most of western Pennsylvania exploded in a roar of outrage.

Within twenty-four hours, Ida Tarbell wrote, more than 3000 oilmen gathered in a protest meeting in the Titusville Opera House. Other mass meetings followed. A Petroleum Producers' Union was formed. Members were pledged not to drill new wells, to restrict oil deliveries and, above all, not to sell to any member of the South Improvement Company. One committee was sent to the state legislature, asking that the company's charter be revoked; another to Congress, asking a Congressional investigation. A petition 93 feet long was sent to the legislature, urging the construction of a free pipeline—a project long blocked by the Pennsylvania Railroad.

Ferreting out the names of those involved in the conspiracy, the oilmen published a list of the principal members of South Improvement and of the railroads that supplied its muscle. Oil shipments were forbidden to any firm on the list, and so united were the independents, so strongly did they enforce their boycott, that Cleveland refineries were forced to close down for lack of oil.

The public clamor was such that a Congressional committee held an investigation in April. Curiously enough, the record was never officially published and distributed as is customary in Congressional inquiries of this kind; every effort was made to hide and bury the details. But persistent Ida Tarbell learned that the Producers' Union had published a local pamphlet containing the testimony, and she managed to locate a few rare copies that still existed in private collections. The disclosures were devastating.

The head of South Improvement had admitted to the Congressional committee that "this charter was a sort of clothes-horse to hang a scheme upon." The contracts with the railroads were exposed; the anticipated $6,000,000 annual kickback admitted. South Improvement officials tried to contend that they were operating only for "the good" of the business, but the chairman of the investigating committee told them: "Your success meant the destruction of every refiner who refused for any reason to join your company, or whom you did not care to have in, and it put the producers entirely in your power. It would make a monopoly such as no set of men are fit to handle."

Such disclosures had created an uproar at the time—a tempest that, unfortunately, had quickly faded and been forgotten. The New York *Tribune* had charged that the South Improvement scheme was just like highway robbery. The company, it thundered, "has simply laid its hand on the throat of the oil traffic with a demand to 'stand and deliver.'"

The public reaction was so unfavorable that the railroads began to regret their corrupt bargain. They tried to bring the independents into the rebate scheme, but these doughty characters would not hear of it. "They demanded open rates, with no rebates to anybody," Ida wrote. So fierce was their hatred of Rockefeller that they refused to meet with him or any other official of South Improvement. They spurned compromise. And so the railroads, shocked and frightened by the storm that had been created, abandoned the sinking ship. They tore up their agreement with South Improvement. They promised that, in the future, oil would be shipped "on a basis of perfect equality," with no special rebates or kickbacks to anyone. It seemed as if the oilmen had won a decisive victory over the monster of monopoly.

But appearances were deceptive. The South Improvement Company had been slain by the united front of the oilmen, but Standard Oil—and Rockefeller—remained. Not understanding, believing in their victory, the oil regions lifted their boycott and began selling oil. And almost the moment that they did, Standard went right back into the rebate-kickback business.

Within two days after the oil war ended, a prominent Cleveland member of the now-defunct South Improvement Company said: "The business *now* will be done by the Standard Oil Company." Events quickly proved him right. Ida Tarbell later commented that Rockefeller had "a mind which, stopped by a wall, burrows and creeps around." In this case, he wasn't the only one who was burrowing and creeping. The railroads had put their sacred honor on the line with oilmen on March 25, 1872; but before the end of April, their word had become worthless. Just so soon and just so fast, in violation of their pledges, did they go right back into the rebate-kickback arrangements with Rockefeller and Standard Oil.

The Rockefeller steamroller now flattened everything in its path. In other articles in her long series, Ida Tarbell described the secret deals and the ruthlessness with which Rockefeller forced competitors into bankruptcy. Pipelines were built to carry oil from the oil regions, as the independent oilmen had desired, but who owned and controlled the pipelines? Rockefeller and Standard Oil. And the rebate-kickback scheme with the railroads worked even more viciously than before.

Records that were sometimes hard to find, but whose accuracy could not be denied, showed what was happening. In March 1879, Standard shipped 18,556,000 barrels of oil—and got a rebate of over 55 cents a gallon, a tidy refund of more than $10,000,000 in a single month. In another month—March of 1878—a competitor, H. C. Ohlen, shipped 29,876 barrels of oil to New York at the "open" rate of $1.20 a barrel. And the railroads paid to Rockefeller 20 cents on every barrel, giving him in a single month $5,975 of his rival's money!

The business throat-cutting took even more vicious forms. In one article, Ida described "The Buffalo Case." This involved an independent refiner by the name of Matthews, who had persisted in bucking Standard Oil. So, one fine night, his refinery was blown up. This effectively put Matthews out of business. An investigation indicated that officials of Standard Oil were responsible. Two of its vice-presidents, John D. Archbold and Henry R. Rogers—the latter Ida's contact at 26 Broadway—had been indicted, along with the local manager of a Standard plant. Archbold and Rogers were acquitted. The local manager was convicted—and then let off by a kindly judge with a ridiculous fine of $250. Matthews sued Standard for damages and finally got a settlement of $85,000; but lawyer's fees and costs ate up most of the money. Matthews was ruined, a Standard competitor eliminated.

In addition to all this, there was bribery. Open, unashamed, naked bribery. When an anti-trust bill was brought up before the Ohio Legislature, it was defeated in a performance in which Standard Oil cash gushed into the pockets of receptive politicians; so great was the scandal that this particular governing body went down in history as the Coal Oil Legislature. When Standard backed Harry B. Payne for U. S. Senator from Ohio, his son, Oliver H. Payne, treasurer of Standard, sat at a desk in a Columbus hotel, bills stacked up in a pile before him, and paid for votes, cash on delivery. In like fashion, newspapers were bought. One Ohio investigation showed that at least 110 Ohio newspapers had signed contracts with Standard to print editorials and "news" furnished by its public relations agency in return for advertising. When the stench of all this finally became too much for Ohio and an anti-trust law was passed, Standard merely transferred its operations to New Jersey. It bought up the entire mayor and council of Bayonne, most of the members of the New Jersey Legislature, and some of the most important statesmen in Washington.

What was the man like who masterminded such devious plots? He was one who considered himself a partner of God. "God gave me my money," he exclaimed on one occasion, and his intent, he said, was to use his wealth according to God's will. Though in after life he did just this, devoting hundreds of millions of dollars to charitable endeavors, men like Hanna and Matthews would hardly have agreed that God had associated himself with Rockefeller's business practices.

Ida Tarbell summed up the oil conflict and the character of Rockefeller himself in these words:

"Thus on the one hand there was an exaggerated sense of personal independence, on the other a firm belief in combination; on one hand a determination to root out the vicious system of rebates practiced by the railway, on the other a determination to keep it alive and profit by it. Those theories which the body of oilmen held as vital and fundamental Mr. Rockefeller and his associates either did not comprehend or were deaf to. This lack of comprehension by many men of what seems to other men to be the most obvious principles of justice is not rare. Many men who are widely known as good share it. Mr. Rockefeller was 'good.' There was no more faithful Baptist in Cleveland than he. Every enterprise of that church he had supported liberally from his youth. He gave to its poor. He visited its sick. He wept with its suffering. Moreover, he gave unostentatiously to many outside charities of whose worthiness he was satisfied. He was simple and frugal in his habits. He never went to the theater, never drank wine. He was a devoted husband, and he gave much time to the training of his children, seeking to develop in them his own habits of economy and charity. Yet he was willing to strain every nerve to obtain for himself special and illegal privileges from the railroads which were bound to ruin every man in the oil business not sharing them with him. Religious emotion and sentiments of charity, propriety and self-denial seem to have taken the place in him of notions of justice and regard for the rights of others."

To get a firsthand glimpse of the man she had so described, Ida herself attended services in the Euclid Avenue Baptist Church in Cleveland one Sunday morning in 1903. She felt a little guilty about it, she afterwards wrote, something like a spy; but she felt she had to see Rockefeller in person. He soon appeared. He was then sixty-four, and power radiated from him. He had a big head, Ida wrote;

a nose that resembled a sharp thorn; lips that were thin slits. He appeared uneasy even in the familiar surroundings of his own church. He twisted his head and peered constantly around him, as if looking for some hidden enemy; but if he recognized the cool young woman who was giving him so much trouble, he gave no sign.

Rockefeller's public attitude was to ignore Ida Tarbell and all her works; but inwardly he and Standard officials seethed. When Rockefeller read Ida's description of the manner in which he had forced Cleveland competitors to the wall and appropriated their businesses, he exploded: "They didn't collapse. They had collapsed before! That's the reason they were so glad to combine their interests with ours, or take the money we offered." Of course, he did not add that he had ruined some and intended to ruin all by the special rebate and kickback favors he got from the railroads—and that this was the reason for the wholesale "collapse" of his competitors in Cleveland.

All of Rockefeller's spleen was vented in private, however. He issued strict orders that no reply was to be made to the articles in *McClure's*. "Not a word," he insisted. "Not a word about that misguided woman!"

Standard officials had to obey his orders, but his loyal son, John D. Rockefeller, Jr., did not. Ida's barrage became too much for the younger Rockefeller, and he finally delivered a speech, "Christianity and Business." In this, by implication, he defended the practices by which Standard had obtained control of 90 per cent of all oil production and distribution in the nation. He compared the great monopoly to the American Beauty rose. "The American Beauty rose," he said, "can be produced in its splendor and fragrance only by sacrificing the early buds which grow up around it." Critics of Standard greeted the comparison with hoots of ridicule.

With tempers flaring, Ida's working relationship with Henry Rogers came to an abrupt end. Her articles, as is so often the case once a muckraker starts muckraking, had touched a kindred soul inside the labyrinth of Standard Oil; and a young shipping clerk, outraged by the skulduggery of his employers, sent her information about the manner in which Standard sabotaged oil shipments of competitors. The railroads under their long-standing agreement with Standard furnished it with all information about oil shipments by its rivals and their destination—and, once Standard got this data, the shipments "were interfered with, their cars sidetracked en route while pressure was brought on buyers to cancel orders."

Ida told Rogers about the charges and asked for Standard's comment.

"Do you have the help of railroad shipping clerks in the operation?" she asked.

"Of course," Rogers replied smoothly, "we do everything we legally and fairly can to find out what our competitors are doing, just as you do in *McClure's Magazine*. But as for any such system of tracking and stopping as you suggest, that is nonsense."

"Well," said Ida, "give me everything you have on this point."

Rogers insisted there was nothing to give; she would have to accept his blanket denial. This, Ida refused to do. She knew that the specific details she had been given were true, and she wrote an article entitled, "Cutting to Kill." With it, *McClure's* reproduced the records sent to Ida by the shipping clerk. Rogers was furious. "Where did you get that stuff?" he asked Ida when they next met.

"Mr. Rogers," Ida replied, "you can't for a moment think that I will tell you where I got it. You will recall my efforts to get from you anything more than a general denial that these practices of espionage so long complained of were untrue, could be explained by legitimate competition. You know this bookkeeping record is true."

That ended Ida's contacts with Standard; there were no more interviews.

Now, as her father had foreseen, Standard counterattacked with viciousness and venom and all the power of its millions. There was the word-of-mouth ridicule. Standard's supporters dubbed Ida "Miss Tarbarrel," a nickname that made Rockefeller cackle with glee. There was the barrage of publicity, belittling her and anointing itself, that Standard's millions bought.

When Ida's history was published in book form, the Oil City *Derrick*, subsidized by Standard, headlined its review: "Hysterical Woman Versus Historical Facts." Gilbert Montague, a Harvard University economist, was so righteously indignant about Ida's exposure of Standard Oil that he wrote a book glorifying Standard and attacking Ida as "a mere gatherer of folklore." It was doubtless only a coincidence that Standard bought and distributed across the nation 5000 copies of this work.

Standard became even more excited about another literary effusion by a "name" writer. In 1910 Elbert Hubbard, one of the best-known essayists of the day, a man with an Horatio Alger cast of mind, turned out a little pamphlet lauding the virtues of centralization which Standard had brought to the oil industry—and lashing out at Ida Tarbell in the most vituperative language anyone had used.

"Ida Tarbell . . . is an honest, bitter, talented, prejudiced and disappointed woman who wrote from her own point of view," Hubbard thundered. "And that view is from the ditch, where her father's wheelbarrow was landed by a Standard Oil tankwagon . . . She shot from cover, and she shot to kill. Such literary bushwhackers should be answered shot for shot."

Ida later wrote that she had been informed "from various interested sources" that Standard ordered the printing of 5,000,000 copies of Hubbard's pamphlet, and Hubbard blanketed the nation with his "bushwhacker" attack on Ida.

Such attempts to belittle her and her work failed. Her *History of Standard Oil* represented the most difficult research task of the muckraker decade, and it carried with it complete conviction. The people of the nation sensed that they had been given the raw truth about the growth and practices of Standard and other great trusts; and Ida Tarbell became the heroine of the hour. S. S. McClure wrote her: "You are today the most generally famous woman in America."

She had set in motion a whole train of events that were to continue long after she herself stopped writing about Standard Oil. Public reaction to her work spurred a whole series of legal attacks on Standard. Three anti-trust suits were brought against Standard in state courts in 1904, four in 1905, fourteen in 1906. The U. S. Bureau of Corporations, headed by James R. Garfield, son of the assassinated President, launched an investigation into Ida's charges; and in 1906 Garfield turned in a report to President Theodore Roosevelt, who by this time had made his famous attack on muckrakers. A cartoon of the period tells the story. It shows Roosevelt scowling and pointing at Garfield as he exclaims: "Oh, you muckraker!" And it shows Garfield holding up a scroll that reads: "Standard Oil is just as naughty as Ida said it was!"

The exposures rolled on and on. One of the most sensational came when newspaper publisher William Randolph Hearst got possession of the so-called "Archbold letters." This was a packet of letters and copies of others taken by a messenger from the files of the Standard vice-president who had been indicted but finally exonerated in the blowing up of the Buffalo refinery. The letters revealed Archbold as Standard's arch-corruptionist. They showed that he had sent checks and certificates of deposit to Congressmen, judges, and such distinguished U. S. Senators as Joseph B. Foraker of Ohio; Joseph W. Bailey of Texas; and Matthew Stanley Quay of Pennsylvania. The letters proved that Archbold had sent checks ranging from $5000 to $15,000 and totaling $44,000 in six months to one Senate leader. This was bribery on a colossal scale; it confirmed everything Ida had written about Standard Oil—and more; and President Roosevelt ordered his Attorney General, Charles J. Bonaparte, to begin an anti-trust action to break up Standard's monopoly of the oil business.

The case dragged through the courts for years, but on May 15, 1911, the U. S. Supreme Court issued a decree ordering the breakup of Standard Oil. The nation's highest court decided, just as Ida had charged, that Standard's object had been "to drive others from the field and exclude them from their right to trade." It ruled that the great holding company must be broken up into separate corporations. At the time, Standard controlled thirty-three companies, and John D. Rockefeller held personally more than one-fourth of all the stock. When these shares were put on the market following the dissolution order, they were priced at $663,000,000.

Such was the result of Ida Tarbell's great effort. Her *History of the Standard Oil Company* has been judged as probably the most sensational series of articles ever published by an American magazine. Professor Allan Nevins, in his two-volume biography of Rockefeller published in 1940, called Ida's book "the most spectacular success of the muckraking period, and its most enduring achievement." And David M. Chalmers, a modern historian of the muckraking era, believes that not even half a century of Rockefeller family philanthropies has managed to erase completely Ida's portrait of Rockefeller as a "cunning, ruthless Shylock."

CHAPTER VI

Upton Sinclair

THE MOST RADICAL of all the muckrakers—the one, as he later wrote, who "never stopped muckraking"—was a writer of fiction. But his was a fiction that was as thoroughly researched and as soundly based on fact as the works of Lincoln Steffens and Ida Tarbell. And one book that he wrote shocked America so profoundly it caused one of the major upheavals of the muckraker decade.

The author was Upton Sinclair. Like many of the other muckrakers, he came from an upper-class American family; but, unlike many of the others, his was a family that had fallen on hard times before he came along. The result was that, as a boy, he learned all about the seamy side of life— and he never forgot it.

Some of Upton Sinclair's ancestors had been captains in the British Navy; and after the family came to America, the naval tradition remained strong for generations. Upton's great-grandfather, Commodore Arthur Sinclair, was a midshipman on the frigate *Constellation* when she fought her famous battle with the *Insurgente* in 1798 during the naval war with France. Commodore Sinclair later commanded warships on the Great Lakes during the War of 1812 and went on to a distinguished career in the Navy.

Three sons of the commodore and four grandsons also became Navy officers, but all resigned their commissions at the outbreak of the Civil War, joining the Confederate Navy. One of Upton Sinclair's uncles fought in the battle between the *Monitor* and *Merrimac* and later served for two years on the famous Confederate raider *Alabama*. Another uncle served on another almost equally famous raider, the *Florida*. Both lived to write accounts of their wartime adventures.

When the South was crushed, the Sinclair family fortunes died with it. Upton Sinclair later wrote that his branch of the family had possessed landed estates and slaves in Virginia before the war, but the slaves had been set free, the homestead burned—all lost. His father, Upton B. Sinclair, was the youngest son of Captain Arthur Sinclair and had been raised in Norfolk, Virginia. He had all the manners—and, unfortunately, many of the weaknesses—of a Southern gentleman in a postwar era that deprived such gentlemen of their heritage of easy living. He became a traveling salesman.

It was for him a hazardous vocation. As Upton Sinclair later wrote in his autobiography, his father had one fatal weakness—drink. Upton explained that "all Southern gentlemen 'drank'" but his father, unfortunately, became a whiskey salesman, a role that required him to hoist a toast

or two with his customers. The hoisting, once started, became ever more frequent and, in the end, unstoppable; and
it was into this family, with the father going down the
road to drink and the mother trying desperately to reform
him, that Upton Sinclair was born in Baltimore in 1878.
"It took my good and gentle-souled father thirty or forty
years to kill himself, and I watched the process week by
week and sometimes hour by hour," he wrote years afterward in explaining why he had become himself a lifelong
prohibitionist.

When Upton's father was sober, he made a good living,
but he was rarely sober for long and Upton's mother waged
a constant battle with poverty. The boy's earliest memories
were of life spent in a succession of dingy boardinghouse
and lodginghouse rooms. He slept on a sofa, if there was
one, and if not "crossways at the foot of my parents' bed."
Sometimes the gaslight would go on in the middle of the
night "and I would start up, rubbing my eyes, and join
in the exciting chase for bedbugs."

There was a constant struggle within the family. When
Upton's father would return from a successful selling ex-
pedition, soused as usual, Upton's mother would rifle his
pockets, squirreling away all the money she could find to
pay for rent and food. Upton Sr. in his befuddled state
never knew just how much he had had in his pockets, but
he felt certain he must have had *something*—and, once he
revived in the morning, there was sure to be a family row.

From all of this, young Upton escaped into literature.
His mother read childhood stories to him, but that did
not satisfy him for long. He had the mind of a genius, and
by the time he was five, he had taught himself to read.

After that, as the family storms swirled around him, he sought escape in reading adventures of his own.

There were, however, two sides to his life. It was not one unrelieved cycle of poverty, but a constant shuttling back and forth between the dregs of lodginghouse life and the luxury of silk sheets and lavish living. His mother's oldest sister had married extremely well. Her husband was John Randolph Bland, who became one of the richest men in Baltimore and the founder of the United States Fidelity and Guaranty Company. Holidays and vacations were spent in the Bland home, and Upton Sinclair, as a boy and growing youth, listened to the idle chatter of many leaders of Baltimore society.

"I breathed that atmosphere of pride and scorn, of values based upon material possessions preserved for two generations or more, and the longer the better," he later wrote. "I do not know why I came to hate it, but I know that I did hate it from my earliest days. And everything in my later life confirmed my resolve never to 'sell out' to that class."

The contrast between poverty and wealth, the desperate struggles of the poor and the snobbishness of the rich, made him ask the persistent question: Why? He began asking it at an early age, and he never stopped. The harsh inequalities and injustices of society, borne in upon him in earliest boyhood, led in the end to his lifelong love affair with socialism.

When Upton was still a small boy, his father moved the family to New York City. There Upton and his mother stayed in a succession of cheap lodginghouses while his father went "on the road," selling his wares. It was here in the city that Upton grew up. He continued his avid reading. He did not go to school until he was ten, and by then he had outread and outlearned most students his own age. There was only one blank; he knew nothing about arithmetic. Once this flaw was remedied, he breezed through eight years of grammar school in two and was ready for high school at the age of twelve. Since he was too young to enter, according to the rules of the day, he had to take the last year of grammar school over again, and this he did at a school on New York's Lower East Side, where his classmates were toughs from the ghettos.

All of these growing years were preparation for the work the man was to do. The constant shuttling between the extremes of life—the boardinghouses, the toughs, the poverty of the East Side; the wealth and luxury of Uncle Bland's home in Baltimore and the superior persons he met there—was to influence virtually every book he was to write; a constant theme was to be the struggle between the haves and the have-nots in American society. And his sympathies were always to be on the side of the have-nots.

His writing career began at an incredibly early age. Upton was only sixteen when a classmate of his at City College, Simon Stern, came in bursting with pride one day, announcing he had written a story that had been accepted "by a monthly magazine published by a Hebrew orphans' home. Straightway I was stirred to emulation. If Simon could write a story, why could not I?" Determined to show he could, Upton wrote a story about a pet bird, dreaming up a plot in which the bird proved the innocence of a colored boy accused of arson. He sent the story off to *Argosy;* it was accepted and he was paid $25—money, with the purchasing power of the dollar what it was in those days, that looked almost like a small fortune to his mother and himself. He was an author!

This first quick success was the only spur he needed. He had been blessed with a lightning fast mind and an incredible fund of energy. Whenever anything interested or excited him, he threw himself into its cause with furious, all-consuming passion. When he read books, he read as if there were not enough hours in the day to devour the literature of the world. When he tried to learn to play the violin, he practiced from breakfast to sundown. When he rode a bicycle, he was possessed by a desire to join the exclusive club of those who had ridden one hundred miles in a day. So now it was with his writing. His active mind drove him to ceaseless activity.

He wrote jokes and sold them to humor magazines for $1 a joke. He wrote stories and hounded editorial offices. Finally, an editor at Street & Smith, publishers of a line of pulp magazines, suggested that he write a fiction series about a cadet at West Point. Though he was only seventeen at the time, Upton Sinclair had no doubt he could do it. Full of the cockiness and confidence that was characteristic of him, he rode his bicycle up to West Point and spent three days taking notes on the dress, drill, and lives of the cadets. Then he bicycled back to the city; and, under the pen name of Lieutenant Frederick Garrison, USA, he wrote some "twenty-five thousand or thirty thousand words" about an imaginary cadet named Mark Mallory. Street & Smith bought the story for $40, and Upton Sinclair's real career was launched. The local color he had put into his account of West Point life was so convincing that the publisher asked if this "new writer" had gone through the military academy. "Yes," replied the editor, "he went through in three days."

For the next three years Upton Sinclair wrote at a fantastic pace. Street & Smith, which was publishing his Mark Mallory series, had a companion series running on the experiences of a plebe at Annapolis. Originally, this series had been written by the editor, but his increasing editorial chores made it impossible for him to keep the series going. Would Upton like to take over the fictional adventures of the naval hero also? Bursting with confidence as always, the young writer spent another three days at the Naval Academy, roaming the halls his ancestors had roamed and soaking up local color. He returned and began to juggle two bylines: now he was Ensign Clarke Fitch, USN; the next moment, Lieutenant Frederick Garrison, USA. He worked at such a feverish pace that he was turning out 8000 words a day, seven days a week, and he was earning enough to support himself and his mother and to pay tuition costs at Columbia University.

It was well that he was, for his father's life was going steadily downhill. He was now getting so drunk that he would never come home, and young Upton would have to search the neighborhood taverns to find him. Ashamed of himself, sensing the gossip of the neighbors, the father wandered farther afield to do his drinking, and Upton had to search the dives of the Bowery to find him—and sometimes came upon him sprawled unconscious in a gutter. When this happened, when his father became too difficult to handle, Upton would deliver him at a hospital door and pay $25 from his slender hoard so that his father could be confined until he dried out.

During these years of deepening family tragedy while

he was turning out potboilers at a furious pace, Upton began to get an inside view of the corrupted society he was later to attack so fiercely in his long stream of novels. He became aware that the city's vicious Tammany Hall machine was bankrolled by the graft it took from dishonest saloonkeepers, gambling dens, and houses of prostitution. He became an eyewitness, too, to the workings of other and more sophisticated forms of what was becoming known as "honest graft." His instructor in this process was his kindly and wealthy Uncle Bland from Baltimore.

Uncle Bland, who took an almost fatherly interest in the boy, came up to New York, seeking some of the city's bonding business. He selected a prominent Tammany Hall leader to be the manager of his New York office; he saw to it that Richard Croker, the all-powerful boss, received "a considerable block of stock." Other Tammany leaders got lesser amounts of stock; the word went out—and Uncle Bland's company got the city's bonding business.

Not satisfied with this, Uncle Bland began to cast eyes on the state, and he played the same game in Albany that he had in New York. To head his Albany office, he selected a man who was about to be elected state treasurer on the Democratic ticket. ". . . And when I asked him what this meant," Upton Sinclair later wrote, "he smiled over the luncheon table and said, 'We businessmen have our little ways of getting what we want.'"

Looking back on this scene when he was in his eighties, Sinclair commented:

"So there I was on the inside of America, watching our invisible government at work. The pattern that my uncle revealed to me in youth served for the arranging of all the facts I later amassed. I have never found anything different, in any part of America; it is thus that big business deals with government at every point where the two come into contact. Every government official in America knows it, likewise every big businessman knows it; talking in private, they joke about it; in public, they deny it with great indignation."

Uncle Bland, Upton wrote, "was one of the kindest and most generous persons I have ever known," and he concluded that "the blame lies with the system"; businessmen either "have to run their businesses that way or give place to somebody who will run it no differently." Such reasoning drove him steadily to the left and prepared the way for his ultimate conversion to the great, unvarying faith of his life—socialism, the alternative, as he saw it, to a system based on unrestrained human greed.

It was now 1900, and Upton Sinclair was tired of dashing off potboilers for Street & Smith. He was fired by the ambition to become a great novelist. He also had an exalted vision of himself—his "Jesus complex," as both friends and critics called it. He saw himself writing novels of such power and scope that they would change and reform the world.

With him, to see was to act. He threw himself into the pursuit of this new vision with the fury and energy of a man possessed. He isolated himself in drafty tents and lonely woodland cabins; he labored fourteen hours a day seven days a week until the superhuman effort ruined his digestion and threatened to break down his health. He married too young—and disastrously; he was consumed by his work and drove his young wife to the brink of suicide; they shivered in drafty shelters in the cold of winter—and almost starved. Once when his wife wanted to brighten their drab quarters with a bright tablecloth, purchased for 30 cents, he made her take it back because they needed that 30 cents for food. Such single-minded pursuit of his dream produced six novels and novelettes between 1900 and 1904, and the entire lot earned him less than $1000 in royalties.

The end of this period of frantic endeavor found Sinclair and his distraught wife living in a board cabin he had helped to build on a hillside outside of Princeton, New Jersey. The last of his stream of unsuccessful novels had been *Manassas,* which he had envisioned as the first of a trilogy dealing with the Civil War. The book sold less than 2000 copies, but it led by an indirect route to the work that was to make him famous.

In the desperate struggle to raise money to finance his writing, Sinclair had met a wealthy Socialist, George D. Herron. Herron had advanced him the $800 that had made the writing of *Manassas* possible; and Upton Sinclair, rebelling at the society he had come to know, seeking an answer to the question "Why?" began to read the writings of Herron and other Socialists and was impressed.

The latter part of 1904 found him reading the Socialist weekly, *Appeal to Reason,* published in Girard, Kansas, and having a circulation of some 500,000 copies. It was just at this time that some 20,000 workers in the Chicago stockyards went on strike. The strike was broken in the most shocking and brutal manner; and Sinclair, rapidly becoming a passionate radical, was outraged. In fiery vein, he wrote a manifesto urging the stockyard workers to fight on and taunting them with the question: "You have lost your strike, and now what are you going to do about it?" He sent this literary call to arms to the *Appeal,* which printed it as a page-one broadside and distributed hundreds of thousands of copies. Elated, the young crusader dashed off another militant diatribe entitled: "Farmers of America, Unite!"

Fred D. Warren, editor of the *Appeal to Reason*, liked this new writer who wrote with such flaming conviction, and he read *Manassas*. He liked the historical novel, and it suggested an idea to him. He wrote Sinclair. *Manassas*, he said, had pictured vividly the struggle to abolish Negro slavery. Why didn't Sinclair do the same thing with a current issue? Why not write a novel about industrial slavery?

The idea appealed to Sinclair at once. Certainly, he would do it, he replied, if the *Appeal* would finance the effort. Warren agreed to advance $500, and, in October, 1904, Sinclair set out for Chicago. His flaming manifestoes in the *Appeal to Reason* had won him friends among the Socialists and laborers in the stockyards, and he intended to use these contacts to find out what life in the great meat-packing houses was really like.

Sinclair lived for seven weeks with the packinghouse workers, and the sights and smells that assaulted him left him "white-faced and thin, partly from undernourishment, partly from horror." In his autobiography, he described his researches in these terms:

"I sat at night in the homes of workers, foreign-born and native, and they told me their stories, one after one, and I made notes of everything. In the daytime I would wander about the yards, and my friends would risk their jobs to show me what I wanted to see. I was not much better dressed than the workers, and found that by the simple device of carrying a dinner pail I could go anywhere.

So long as I kept moving, no one would heed me. When I wanted to make careful observations, I would pass again and again through the same room.

"I went about the district, talking with lawyers, doctors, dentists, nurses, policemen, politicians, real estate agents—every sort of person. I got my meals at the University Settlement, where I could check my data with the men and women who were giving their lives to this neighborhood . . ."

Sinclair checked and rechecked his facts, careful to be accurate, guarding against the danger of overreacting to what were to him new and horrifying scenes. Then, with his data confirmed in every way he could imagine, he began to worry about his plot. He had facts, but no characters. How was he to write a novel? He was worrying about this one Sunday afternoon when he saw a wedding party drawing up in carriages to the rear door of a saloon. He slipped in and joined the party. All that afternoon and far into the night, he made himself as inconspicuous as possible as he observed and committed to memory every detail of the festivities. And the first chapter of the book he was to call *The Jungle* began to take shape in his head.

Back in Princeton, he isolated himself in the small work-cabin, eight feet wide by ten feet long that he had built himself the year before. The cabin was perched on a hillside and heated by a small, round coal stove; and in this, on Christmas Day, 1904, Upton Sinclair went to work on *The Jungle*. He worked as he himself later wrote for three months "incessantly. I wrote with tears and anguish, pouring into the pages all the pain that life had meant to me." This time, when he was finished, he knew he had something that would be read.

The Jungle is perhaps the most brutal novel ever written in America. It is one long scream of pain and tragedy. Its central figure is Jurgis Rudkus, a Lithuanian peasant, and the secondary characters are members of his family and his friends. All are immigrants lured to what Sinclair called "Packingtown" by the false promises of packinghouse agents about the high wages to be earned there. Not knowing the language, not knowing the country or the circumstances, these workers are taken advantage of on every hand. Jurgis has to pay graft to get and keep his job in the packinghouse; a real-estate man cheats him by selling him a house on the installment plan, with fine clauses written into a contract he cannot read or understand—clauses that will cost him his house. Jurgis is forced to work at a frantic, speeded-up pace and inevitably is injured; he and his family contract horrible diseases in the insanitary conditions of the packinghouses; he is laid off and blacklisted, then sent to jail, when it all becomes too much for him and he smashes the face of a brutal boss. One by one, Jurgis and his friends are crushed. The men, worked beyond endurance, worn out before their time, are cast out to starve; the women are forced into prostitution. In the end, Jurgis, broken and alone, wanders in a hopeless mire of despair until he spies a great new hope, until he becomes convinced that only socialism can remake and save so hideous a world.

Upton Sinclair, in telling this story, had hoped to convert Americans to socialism, but that was not what his book did. Readers didn't care about the political philosophy imbedded in his message; what shocked, what stunned them was his description of the incredible abuses in the packinghouses—and the revolting details about the meat they were eating. As Sinclair himself later said: "I aimed at the public's heart and by accident I hit it in the stomach."

The sensation was caused by a little more than a dozen pages of descriptive writing. These depicted conditions in the packinghouses as Sinclair had found them in his on-the-spot researches. He wrote that the best meats were sent abroad because England, France, and Germany—especially, Germany—had inspection systems that rejected the kind of poisonous meat products that were being palmed off on the American people as choice foods. Diseased, dying, even long-dead cattle were carved up and sold to the American public as prime meat. Any inspector who tried to interfere with this system did not last long, Sinclair wrote.

He told of a case where a physician "made the discovery that the carcasses of steers which had been condemned as tubercular by government inspectors, and which therefore contained ptomaines, which are deadly poisons, were left upon an open platform and carted away to be sold in the city, and so he insisted that these carcasses be treated with an injection of kerosene—and was ordered to resign the same week! So indignant were the packers that they went farther, and compelled the mayor to abolish the whole bureau of inspection; so that since then there has not been even a pretense of any interference with the graft. There was said to be two thousand dollars a week hush money from the tubercular steers alone, and as much again from the hogs which had died of cholera on the trains, and which you might see any day being loaded into box cars and hauled away to a place called Globe, in Indiana, where they made a fancy grade of lard."

In Packingtown a corny jest made the rounds—"that they

use everything in the pig except the squeal." Hams that were spoiled "with an odor so bad a man could hardly bear to be in the room with them" were pumped full of a strong pickle to destroy the odor—and then were sold to the public. The most putrid meats were sent along to the sausage-grinding department, where they were thrown into hoppers with a half-ton of other meats, were ground up by rapidly whirling cutters and were spewed out, their odor lost and their deadly disease-carrying potential disguised. Sinclair wrote:

". . . There was never the least attention paid to what was cut up for sausages; there would come all the way back from Europe old sausage that had been rejected, and that was moldy and white—it would be dosed with borax and glycerine, and dumped into the hoppers, and made over again for home consumption. There would be meat that had tumbled out on the floor, in the dirt and sawdust, where the workers had tramped and spit uncounted billions of consumption germs. There would be meat stored in great piles in rooms; and the water from leaky roofs would drip over it, and thousands of rats would race about on it. It was too dark in these storage places to see well, but a man could run his hand over these piles of meat and sweep off handfuls of dried dung of rats. These rats were nuisances, and the packers would put poisoned bread out for them, and they would die, and then the rats, bread and meat would go into the hoppers together. This is no fairy story and no joke . . ."

Horrible as all this was, Sinclair topped it with a final disclosure. He described tank rooms full of steam in which men labored on slippery floors processing the meat. Since "there were open vats upon the level of the floor," the "peculiar trouble" of these workers "was that they fell into the vats; and when they were fished out, there was never enough of them left to be worth exhibiting. Sometimes they would be overlooked for days, till all but the bones of them had gone out to the world as Anderson's Pure Leaf Lard!"

By the time Upton Sinclair finished writing *The Jungle* he was physically exhausted. A relative offered him a pass on a steamer to Savannah. He took it, went on to the Florida coast, and spent two weeks surf fishing and wandering the beaches. In the meantime, the first installments of his novel appeared in *Appeal to Reason,* and the first shock waves of reaction began to creep across the land. Refreshed from his short vacation, Sinclair returned home and spent the rest of the spring and summer rewriting and putting the manuscript into shape for publishing in book form.

Now came trouble. George P. Brett of the Macmillan Company had read the first chapters of *The Jungle* and had been so impressed that he had given Sinclair a book advance of $500. But the more he read the more shocked Brett became. He finally called Sinclair into his office and asked him "to cut some of the 'blood and guts' from the book; nothing so horrible had ever been published in America—at least not by a reputable concern." Sinclair refused to make the changes. He discussed his problem with Lincoln Steffens, who seemed to side with Brett. "It is useless to tell things that are incredible, even though they may be true," Steffens advised. But Sinclair could not bring himself to soften his work; "I had to tell the truth, and let people make of it what they would."

Four other publishers turned down his masterwork, and

by this time Sinclair was furious—and determined. He would publish the book himself if no publisher dared. The sympathetic editor of *Appeal to Reason* gave him space to state his case, and Jack London, then at the height of his fame as a novelist, wrote what Sinclair called "a rousing manifesto" urging the socialist movement to rally behind the book. It was, London declared, "the *Uncle Tom's Cabin* of wage slavery. It is alive and warm. It is brutal with life. It is written of sweat and blood, and groans and tears."

Sinclair followed this by asking readers of the *Appeal* to pay $1.20 in advance for a "Sustainer's Edition" of the book, and in a couple of months some $4000 poured in— "more money than I had been able to earn in the past five years," Sinclair wrote. With such a volume of assured sales in hand, he offered the book to Doubleday, Page & Co. He was called in for a conference with Walter H. Page, the editor, whom he found "extremely kind and extremely naïve; being good himself, he believed that other people were good . . ." This kindly man was anxious to harm no one unjustly and so he sent proofs of the book to James Keeley, managing editor of the Chicago *Tribune*, for his comment. Keeley turned the task over to a reporter who was supposed to be an expert on the stockyards—and back came a thirty-two page report tearing *The Jungle* to shreds. "I sat down to luncheon with the firm, at which this report was produced," Sinclair wrote, "and I talked for two or three hours exposing its rascalities. I persuaded the firm to make an investigation of their own, and so they sent out a young lawyer, and the first person this lawyer met in the yards was a publicity agent of the packers. The lawyer mentioned *The Jungle*, and the agent said, 'Oh, yes, I know that book. I read the proofs of it and prepared a thirty-two page report for James Keeley of the *Tribune*.'"

With this attempted fix exposed, Doubleday sent out one of its editors, Isaac F. Marcosson, who confirmed everything Sinclair had written—and more. Marcosson later reported: "I was able to get a Meat Inspector's badge, which gave me access to the secret confines of the meat empire. Day and night I prowled over its foul-smelling domain, and I was able to see with my own eyes much that Sinclair had never even heard about."

Convinced of Sinclair's accuracy, Doubleday published *The Jungle*. And a hurricane of reaction shook a horrified nation.

Sinclair's disclosures were page one news in almost every newspaper in the land. In Washington, President Roosevelt began to get one hundred letters a day asking about this horror story and demanding to know what he proposed to do about it.

This explosive reaction was the result of several factors. The timing was right for public acceptance of Sinclair's message—and for the shock, anger, and demand for action that followed. The work of other and earlier muckrakers had prepared the way; the public had been conditioned to accept the idea that the power complexes of the time were ruthless and corrupt. In addition, there was one vivid, searing public memory. During the Spanish-American War in 1898, the great packinghouses had shipped our servicemen meat products that were so foul they became known as "embalmed beef." Disease had swept the ranks; death rates had soared. It was later reported, with no exaggeration, that more American fighting men had been killed off by the meat packers than by Spanish bullets.

Yet, as *The Jungle* demonstrated, this scandal had changed nothing; the packers had not been shamed into reform. They were still serving up to the American people the same kind of diseased meats that had killed off our soldiers in Florida and Cuba.

One gets a vivid sense of the resulting public outrage by reading some of the comments of the time. One of the foremost social critics of the age was Chicago's Finley Peter Dunne. Writing in the Irish brogue of an imaginary character he named "Mr. Dooley," Dunne's biting, satirical humor shriveled his targets. Here is the way he described President Roosevelt's reaction to *The Jungle:*

"Tiddy was toying with a light breakfast an' idly turnin' over th' pages if th' new book with both hands. Suddenly he rose fr'm th' table, an' cryin': 'I'm pizened,' begun throwin' sausages out iv th' window. Th' ninth wan sthruck Sinitor Biv'ridge on th' head an' made him a blond. It bounced off, exploded, an' blew a leg off a secret-service agent, an' th' scattered fragmints desthroyed a handsome row iv ol' oak-trees. Sinitor Biv'ridge rushed in, thinkin' that th' Prisident was bein' assassynated by his devoted followers in th' Sinit, an' discovered Tiddy engaged in hand-to-hand conflict with a potted ham. Th' Sinitor fr'm Injyanny, with a few well-directed wurruds, put out th' fuse an' rendered the missile harmless. Since thin th' Prisidint, like th' rest iv us, has become a viggytaryan . . ."

In similar vein, a parody on a familiar childhood rhyme appeared in the press. It read:

> Mary had a little lamb,
> And when she saw it sicken,
> She shipped it off to Packingtown,
> And now it's labeled chicken.

The packing industry struck back, hard and viciously. With its enormous financial resources and its influence, it was able to win itself favorable publicity. Its greatest coup was a series of articles in *The Saturday Evening Post* by J. Ogden Armour, head of the famous Armour meat-packing house. Armour's former secretary, George Horace Lorimer, was editor of the *Post*, and the series described a meat industry noble in motive and producing only the purest products. Sinclair was incensed. Though Armour had not referred to him or *The Jungle*, the aim obviously was to discredit him; and so, boiling with indignation, he sat down and wrote all of one long night, producing an 8000-word article entitled "The Condemned Meat Industry."

He took the article to *Everybody's Magazine* and went into a huddle with the periodical's publisher, editors—and lawyers. The lawyers, of course, wanted proof of the dynamite in Sinclair's charges since he was now writing fact, not fiction. Fortunately for himself, Sinclair had abundant documentation. In Chicago he had met "a wild, one-eyed Irishman who had been a foreman on Armour's killing beds and had told under oath the story of how the condemned carcasses, thrown into the tanks to be destroyed, were taken out at the bottom of the tanks and sold in the city for meat. The Armours had come to him, and offered him $5000 to retract his story; by advice of a lawyer he accepted the money and put it in a bank for his little daughter, and then made another affidavit, telling how he had been bribed and why. I had both these affidavits; also I had the court records of many pleas of guilty that Mr. Armour and his associates had entered in various states to the charge of selling adulterated meat products." Convinced,

Everybody's accepted and published Sinclair's devastating reply to Armour.

Still the meat industry was in no mood to surrender, to admit the facts, to reform itself. All its resources were marshalled in an attempt to demolish its critic. Such important newspapers as the Chicago *Tribune* and the Boston *Transcript* rallied to the defense of the packers and attacked Sinclair in news stories and editorials. Huge and expensive advertisements appeared in the press lauding the great meat-packing industry. Every effort was made to portray Sinclair as some irresponsible sensation-seeker, and all the pressure money could bring to bear was exerted to block any attempt in Congress to establish federal control and regulation of the meat industry.

The uproar in the nation was so great that President Roosevelt wrote Sinclair he was asking the Department of Agriculture to investigate. Sinclair replied that this "was like asking a burglar to determine his own guilt." Teddy Roosevelt then invited him to a luncheon at the White House, where Sinclair met James R. Garfield and other members of the President's inner circle. During a discussion of the meat-packing issue, the President said: "Mr. Sinclair, I bear no love for these gentlemen, for I ate the meat they canned for the Army in Cuba."

The talk turned to the political situation in Washington, and Sinclair was amazed at Roosevelt's frankness. The President was soon to denounce the whole tribe of exposé writers as muckrakers, but nothing that the muckrakers themselves ever charged could equal the things Roosevelt said as he ran down the list of the members of the U. S. Senate. He denounced them one by one. He was especially vehement about Senator Eugene Hale of Maine, whom he called "the Senator from the Shipbuilding Trust"; and Sinclair made notes of the conversation immediately afterward. "If you want to get the full effect of it," he wrote years later, "sit at a table, clench your fist, and hit the table at every accented syllable: 'The most in-*nate*-ly and es-*sen*-tial-ly mal-*e*-vo-lent *scoun*-drel that God *Almight-y ev*-er put on *earth!*'" Recalling this performance and the way Roosevelt soon defended in public the very Senators he had so denounced in private, Sinclair later commented that "this experience did not increase my respect for the game of politics as played in America."

On his return from the presidential luncheon in Washington, Sinclair found waiting for him "a business gentleman with dollar signs written all over him, trying to interest me in a proposition to establish an independent packing company and market my name and reputation to the world. This gentleman haunted my life for a month, and before he got through he had raised his bid to $300,000 in stock. I have never been sure whether it was a real offer, or a well-disguised attempt to bribe me."

The tempest stirred up by *The Jungle* raged on. Roosevelt's investigating commissioners wanted Sinclair to go to Chicago with them, but he had no desire to repeat his work. Instead, now having money, he sent out two Socialists whom he had come to know in Trenton, Ella Reeve Bloor and her husband, and he paid their expenses of $1000 out of his own pocket. In the thirties, Mrs. Bloor was to become known as "Mother Bloor," an active Communist and the head of Communist cells, but at this time her value was that she and her husband knew many of the immigrant workers in the Chicago packing plants. She put Roosevelt's investigators in touch with potential witnesses;

and this official probe confirmed, just as the earlier Double-day inquiry had, virtually everything Sinclair had written, "except that I was not able to produce legal proof of men falling into vats and being rendered into pure leaf lard. There had been several cases, but always the packers had seen to it that the widows were returned to the old country."

Roosevelt, the clever politician, held up publication of the report, hoping to get a reform bill passed by Congress while making as few enemies as possible. But the packers themselves prevented this. Behind the scenes, they worked feverishly to block any federal regulation of their industry. It seemed as if they might succeed; and so Sinclair, with the quiet consent of Roosevelt's own investigators, tipped off the New York *Times* to the importance of Mr. and Mrs. Bloor. The *Times* broke the story; Roosevelt had to release the scathing official report that condemned the packing industry; and another wave of indignation swept the land.

Sinclair decided to counteract the public relations efforts of the packers by becoming a volunteer publicity agent for federal legislation. He opened an office in a couple of rooms in a New York hotel and gave out interviews and wrote press releases until he "was dizzy." It was sometimes two o'clock in the morning before he finished his labors.

He was now famous. The New York *Evening World* declared: "Not since Byron awoke one morning to find himself famous has there been such an example of world-wide celebrity won in a day by a book as has come to Upton Sinclair." *The Jungle* was a best-seller in England and America for six months, and it was being translated into seventeen languages. In England, Winston Churchill, later to become Prime Minister of his embattled nation in World War II, praised *The Jungle* as a masterwork. "This terrible book . . . pierces the thickest skull and most leathery heart," he wrote.

It had not pierced the thickest skulls and most leathery hearts among the meat packers, but it had had its effect on the American people. Meat sales were cut in half, and even a Congress that could be bribed or influenced on most issues became convinced that it must heed the public storm and save the packers from themselves. The result was that, only six short months after the publication of *The Jungle*, Congress passed the Pure Food and Drug Act and the Beef Inspection Act. The effect was to abolish the worst abuses Upton Sinclair had discovered and to assure the public it would no longer be poisoned by the meat it bought and ate. In his message to Congress on December 3, 1907, President Roosevelt claimed that the law, though it had been in effect only a short time, had already greatly benefited both the public and reputable packers who, he said, "are better off under the law than they were without it."

Privately, Roosevelt wanted a little quiet, and so he sent a message to Sinclair through F. N. Doubleday. "Tell Sinclair to go home and let me run the country for a while," he said.

Upton Sinclair was not a man to take such advice. He was a man with a mission—to reform all America. He suggested to *Everybody's* a series of articles exposing the conditions under which children worked in industry. The magazine thought this was a great idea and commissioned Sinclair to do a series of eight or ten articles. The writer threw himself into his new task with all of his usual, all-consuming energy. He went first to the glass factories of southern New Jersey, and there he watched little boys of ten or twelve working all night in front of red-hot furnaces. They were so exhausted when their long trick was done that they were ready to collapse. One boy, staggering toward his home at daybreak, fell asleep on the railroad tracks— and was run over by a train and killed.

From New Jersey, Sinclair went to the Allegheny steel country of Pennsylvania, "the real headquarters of American wage slavery in those old days," he later wrote. Everywhere he went, he lived in the homes of the workers, ate their meals, talked to them and got their stories. And what he discovered was so horrible that, even in those free-wheeling muckraking days, *Everybody's* refused to publish it. "So I had to rest, whether I would or not," he wrote.

Much of the material he gathered he used as background in later novels, but none ever had the impact of *The Jungle*—that "terrible book" that had shocked the nation, had reformed the meat-packing industry, and had given the American people purer food.

CHAPTER VII

Charles Edward Russell

CHARLES EDWARD RUSSELL was an unusual muckraker—a reluctant muckraker, a muckraker by accident. And yet he was one whose whole life experience drove him relentlessly toward membership in the band of crusading journalists who were exposing the flaws in American society and demanding reform.

Russell was born in Davenport, Iowa, in 1860. His father was editor and part-owner of the morning Davenport *Gazette*, a stanch Republican—indeed, one of the founders of the Republican Party. But the party, like the times, had changed.

It is not often recognized today, but it is nevertheless a fact, that the Republican Party was originally a radical party. It was not only opposed to slavery, but it denounced many forms of injustice and stood for broad reforms. After the Civil War, it became the dominant political party of the nation, and it quickly became utterly conservative—the favorite party of the trusts and big business interests that were changing the face of America and coming to dominate American life.

In the Russells, both father and son, there lived, however, the ideals of free and independent Westerners who had pioneered the prairie lands and had seen in the formation of the Republican Party the political fulfillment of their principles. The party might change, but they would not. They belonged to an independent breed, their faith rooted, as that of the founding fathers had been, in individual man; their concern justice and opportunity for this man—their distrust, their enmity aroused by forces that would crush him and reduce him to a cipher in the cause of big enterprise, usually Eastern big business enterprise.

It was this devotion to the Westerner's freewheeling individualism and to the original tenets of the Republican Party that was to lead the father to business ruin—and the son to rebellion and a prominent muckraking role.

In his autobiography, Charles Edward Russell described his first adventure in journalism. As a boy, he helped out around the *Gazette* plant, his principal chore the distasteful task of mixing up buckets of paste and wrapping and labeling copies of the paper as they came off the old flatbed press. He was so employed when chance placed a pen in his hand.

Davenport at the time had a volunteer fire department, but no electric alarm system. Two companies began to compete with city officials to install such a system, and Russell's father smelled out the odor of graft in the pending deal. He wrote a long article exposing the situation, but unfortunately, just as the press started to roll, a prankster engaged in some pressroom tomfoolery accidentally flipped one of Russell's glue brushes on to the type. The roller of the press crushed brush and type, leaving a gap of several paragraphs in the story. The original copy could not be found and so the type could not be reset.

"Leave it to me," young Russell said. "I know what my father thinks about this business. Get me some paper."

In a few minutes, he dashed off enough prose to fill the gap in the type. The result: two threats of libel suits within twenty-four hours and "an irate and red-faced gentleman of German persuasion puffing up the office stairs, a stick in hand to commit assault and battery . . ." As Russell explained, he had "not spared the epithets," and his brief contribution rang with words like "thieves" and "scoundrels." The outcome, however, was gratifying. The grafting deal his father had smelled out was stopped dead.

Perhaps convinced by this result that he had a young genius on his hands, Russell's father sent the boy East to get an education. The school selected was St. Johnsbury Academy in the town of that name in northern Vermont, not far from the Canadian border. Here the boy not only got an education, he began to see at firsthand some of those iniquities in American life that were to turn him eventually into a muckraker.

His early rebellion was fostered by the strict religious regimen of the school: prayers every morning, compulsory church services every Sunday, students locked into their rooms at 8 o'clock every night, all diversions frowned upon and dancing a cardinal sin. "The whole thing reeked of piety; aggressive, militant, grim, implacable," Russell later wrote.

As he rebelled against the puritanical strictness of the school, so the independent Westerner in him also rebelled at the atmosphere in St. Johnsbury itself. He quickly learned that this beautiful Vermont town, like many another in New England, was run much like a feudal barony. "The baronial family lived in a castle on the height; the townspeople kow-towed below," he recalled years afterward. "The place was the site of the Fairbanks scale factory; members of the Fairbanks family were the barons; in effect their word was law. Without assuming any ostensible place or reachable responsibility in the government, they ruled it absolutely. Whatever they wanted, they had, and no man made question thereof . . .

"The whole thing struck my Western soul into dismay and then into rebellion, the more, perhaps, because the two forms of feudalism that gravelled me were really identical. It was the Fairbanks family that sustained, managed and inspired the Academy and was responsible for the puritanical lunacies practiced there. It was also the Fairbanks family that ruled St. Johnsbury with an unassailable sway. Privilege building toward autocracy—it was the old story . . . In the West we knew that some men were richer than others, but had any one of the richer assumed dictatorial powers because of his wealth he would have been torn out of his estate. Here the thing that among my people would have staged a riot was accepted, tolerated, and even defended."

The evil of what Russell called the great Trickle and Filter Theory of Social Existence—the idea that extreme wealth concentrated in a few hands was really a fine thing because the wealthy would spend and some of their wealth would trickle down into the pockets of the poor—was symbolized for Russell in the life story of one striking, never-forgotten man whom he came to know well in St. Johnsbury. He was Jim Dow, a machinist in the Fairbanks works, the man who ran the machine that notched the scales. A hairbreadth error on his part could ruin five hundred scales; the factory, in essence, depended upon his skill.

"Yet when at the end of the week he had paid the slender stipend due at the boardinghouse he had left for his clothing and all other expenses the sum of four dollars," Russell wrote. "There were stockholders of the company that contributed nothing to the enterprise, not even their gracious presence, and drew from it in a week more than Jim Dow received in a year." And this was so despite the fact that Jim Dow was a cultured man, intelligent, educated, even brilliant—a man of far greater worth than scores of his so-called betters in the Fairbanks barony.

Jim Dow had had only a basic public school education, but he had not stopped there. He had continued all his life the process of reading and self-education until he had become, Russell wrote, "one of the best-read men I have ever known . . . He had even the voice of the highly educated man, soft, melodious, restrained, and he won to a philosophy of life that highly educated men might not always attain." He had never married "because he felt that with his slender wage, marriage would be unfair to the woman." On his four dollars a week, he could save nothing; it cost every penny to keep himself clean and neatly dressed and to provide for "the cultural enjoyments that were his real life." Already on the downhill side of life when young Russell knew him, Jim Dow faced the future with no illusions. "I suppose I shall notch beams until I am too old to run the machine," he said. "Then what? Old men's home I suppose. A man must take what comes to him."

Charles Edward Russell could not accept the idea that "a man must take what comes to him." With his Western sense of independence, he rebelled at a system rife with such obvious injustices—a system that considered Jim Dow a chattel of little worth, to be used, burned out, and cast aside on a human scrap heap.

Rebellion burned in the heart of the young scholar whose first journalistic effort had flamed with words like "thieves" and "scoundrels." Returning home to Iowa, he saw on every hand more evidence of a callous and brutal system. The Republican Party, as the vehicle of big business, had imposed upon the nation fantastically high protective tariff rates. In some industries, tariff rates had soared to 75 per cent. This meant that American manufacturers could charge 75 per cent more for their wares than would have been the case could American consumers have purchased goods freely imported from abroad. This high tariff wall created millionaires in wholesale lots back in the industrial East; but out in the farming West, Russell's native country, the system impoverished even the most industrious.

The farmer had no protection for his products. He had to compete in a free world market. As a result, the prices he got for his produce were hammered down to levels of bare subsistence. Russell wrote: "The average Iowa farm in those days was a quarter section, or 160 acres, of phenomenally rich earth, and the net result of a year's grinding labor upon it was relatively less than a French peasant reaped from a patch of perhaps a twentieth of that area. Year after year the Iowa farmer turned the black loam, sowed the seed, watched his crop to an abundant harvesting, took it with expectancy to the market and came away with enough to pay the interest upon his mortgage and little besides." And in bad times, in depressions—many brought on by the speculative excesses of Eastern capital—the farmer could not even get enough money to pay the interest on his mortgage. Then he lost his farm.

Moved by the plight of the farmer, coming from a family with resources sufficient to let him indulge himself in causes, Russell threw himself into the free trade movement. In 1881, with Henry J. Philpott, editor of *The Leader* in Des Moines, he formed the Iowa State Free Trade League, the first of its kind in the nation. Philpott had made an intensive study of the protective tariff system and had become convinced that "the idea of using government for personal ends, originating in the Protective theory, had spread through the nation and . . . was turning it into a society chiefly composed of plunderers and the plundered."

Russell through his association with Philpott came to know many of the dissidents in the West. He became involved in a number of reform movements and came to know well the former Union Army general, James B. Weaver. In 1892 Weaver became the presidential candidate of a radical third party—the People's or the Populist Party—and he shocked the conservative elements of the nation by polling more than one million popular votes and carrying six Western states.

Before this happened, however, the Russell family fortunes had been ruined. Russell's father had continued to run the Davenport *Gazette* in courageous fashion, adhering to the original principles of the Republican Party he had helped to found. These principles put him on the side of the farmer and the average, humble citizen; and they pitted

129

him against the rising forces of business autocracy that was establishing virtual monopolies over many areas of American life. This was a collision course, but it was one that avoided disaster until Russell's father committed the cardinal indiscretion: he began attacking the railroad interests. And the railroads in the 1880s, as Russell was to write, "were the government."

They were unchecked, unregulated, accountable to no one. They could charge whatever freight rates they pleased. They gave rebates to favored customers like John D. Rockefeller and Standard Oil, and they assessed ruinous rates against all who opposed them. They wooed politicians, judges, juries with free passes to travel anywhere they liked. They poured out money in political campaigns and managed to rig the count against any candidate who dared to oppose them. They acquired such power, Russell wrote, that they were able "to corrupt government, to silence and control the press with passes, to gag criticism with rebates and privileges"; and the result was that they created, in effect, "in the heart of the Republic an absolute monarchy."

When Russell's father challenged this monarchy, disaster swiftly followed. The railroad simply refused to transport the coal he needed to keep his plant and presses running. To avoid closing down, he tried the desperate expedient of taking wagons out into the country, where he and his workers dug a thin vein of nearly worthless surface coal. Even this was not to be permitted. The railroad interests, with their enormous power in the courts, brought a minority stockholder's suit against him, obtained a judgment and seized his paper. "The *Gazette,* which had always been regarded as a family heirloom, was suddenly wrenched from his grasp and the whole Russell tribe found itself slung upon the sidewalks," the son later wrote.

Forced to scrabble for a living, young Russell became a reporter. He went to New York, where he joined the staff of the *Commercial Advertiser* and later that of the New York *World*. He covered the slums of the Lower East Side, reporting on the horrors of tenement life and on the crimes that flourished there; the *World* sent him to Chicago to cover the Haymarket riot in 1886, one of the most violent of the times; and through it all what impressed him always were the growing inequities in American society—the callousness and indifference of the idle super-rich; the disease, squalor, and degradation in which the huddled tenement masses dragged out their short and miserable lives.

In twenty years as a journalist, Russell rose to the top level of his profession. He became city editor of the *World*, directing one of the greatest newspaper staffs ever assembled. Later he went to Chicago and helped William Randolph Hearst establish the Chicago *American*. As a well-salaried executive, he saved enough money to make himself financially independent; and so in 1902, just as the muckraker age was dawning, he cut his newspaper ties and became a free-lance writer.

Now in his early forties, Russell was at the height of his powers. He was a writer of considerable literary skill; a Westerner still guided by his region's rugged individualism; a journalist drawing on twenty years' experience of American life and government on every level. The result was writing that was informed by insight and that was vigorous, powerful, at times devastating.

Russell was to write more muckraking articles—articles of greater scope and variety—than any other journalist of his time. He covered in his one person the whole span of the muckraking effort; there was hardly an issue that he did not deal with in his own thorough and principled way. In the end, he was to play a key role in the suppression and the downfall of the whole effort because his ideas and his exposures hit the all-powerful such tremendous blows. Yet, peculiarly enough, when he retired from the newspaper world, nothing was further from his thoughts. He envisioned a peaceful retirement in which he would write poetry and improve his piano playing.

All of these plans were blown out the window by sheer accident. Late in 1904 the Interstate Commerce Commission held a series of hearings on the Chicago packinghouse situation. The hearings focused, not as Upton Sinclair was to do on the quality of meat products, but on the economics of the industry. The probe disclosed the existence of a great beef trust, comprised of the major packers, that wielded dictatorial power, much as Standard Oil had, through conspiratorial arrangements with the railroads.

The great packinghouses had gotten together and bought up all the yellow-painted refrigerator cars then in existence. The railroads paid the packers for the "use" of these cars that ran over their own rail lines. Such payments for "use" naturally reduced freight charges to members of the combine—and anyone who didn't belong was soaked at a ruinous rate. By their stranglehold on refrigerated rail shipments, the packers were able to extend their grasp into other fields; shipments of vegetables, fruits, any kind of perishable products came under their heel. The result: the packers were enriched, prices were forced ever higher, the public was gouged.

Such was the situation when Erman J. Ridgway, editor

of *Everybody's,* one of the foremost muckraking magazines, decided to run an article on the machinations of the beef trust. The key witness before the Interstate Commerce Commission had been M. J. W. Midgeley, the most famous expert on railroad rates in the nation. Ridgway thought Midgeley might be able to do an article for *Everybody's,* and he wired his friend, Charles Edward Russell, to do him a favor and contact Midgeley.

As the former editor of Hearst's Chicago *American,* Russell had been aware of some of the packinghouse scandals, but he had no idea that the kind of conditions Upton Sinclair was discovering existed in the plants. He had no thought, therefore, of becoming involved himself when he went to see Midgeley with Ridgway's proposition. Midgeley, it turned out, was too busy to write the article; and Russell, his interest aroused, wandered over to a hearing room in which the Interstate Commerce Commission was holding yet another session in its packinghouse probe.

Several farmers testified. They described how the conspiracy between the beef trust and the railroads was practically ruining them. The freight charges imposed on their shipments of cattle and produce were so outrageous that all of their profits were eaten away, and they faced ruin. As he listened, Russell's deepest sympathies were engaged. Here again was man—the individual, hard-working man in whom he intensely believed—being victimized, ground down by all-powerful and greedy interests. Enraged, Russell determined on the spot to write the beef trust article himself.

He threw himself into the task with all his old, highly trained reportorial skill. He began to dig for facts, and he soon found the facts were so abundant they could not be crammed into a single article; he would have to write a

133

whole series to do them justice. Knowing that every avenue of information that could be closed would be closed the instant the packers sensed what he was up to, he decided not to write a line until he had gathered all the data he could. A friend who had access to some inside information in the stockyards helped him. There had been some fallings out among the packers which had led to law suits, and Russell dug up much revealing information from court records and the ICC hearings.

Putting it all together, Russell produced a series, "The Greatest Trust in the World," that began running in *Everybody's* early in 1905. Russell's approach was different than Upton Sinclair's. He concentrated on the economic aspects of the beef trust, on the way in which it victimized the farmer and crushed all competition; he did not picture, as Sinclair was doing almost by accident, the disgusting and diseased food that was poisoning the American people. But Russell's series, reinforcing Sinclair's disclosures in *The Jungle,* attracted wide attention and helped to whip up public passion against the packers. Almost instantly, Russell became a prime target of the moneyed interests. Detectives were put on his trail; attempts were made to involve him in personal scandal. Conservatives assailed his motives, and the packing trust bought advertising space in Western newspapers to denounce his charges that suicides, banking failures and the paradox of abundant crops, impoverished farmers and high consumer prices could be laid at its door.

The uproar launched Russell on a new career he had never anticipated. Though the names of Steffens and Tarbell were to become more famous and last longer in public memory, Charles Edward Russell was considered in his time the peer of them all. He wrote from conscience and deep feeling. Skilled in research, he was always responsible and made exceptionally few mistakes. And his writing reflected his complete sincerity. He deeply believed in the virtue, even the necessity for muckraking. He felt that democracy could survive only if the people could be kept constantly informed. There are inevitable abuses that arise in any system; there are always those greedy for wealth and power whose ambitions know no limit and who reach for dictatorial authority. They could be restrained, the democratic system could be made to work, Russell felt, only through the constant vigilance of the muckraker, only if the muckraker kept a full and blinding spotlight on abuses and aroused the public to correct them.

His thinking is perhaps best disclosed in one passage of his autobiography. One of Russell's closest friends was David Graham Phillips, a journalist reared in Indiana who was to produce some of the most flaming articles and fiction of the muckraking age. Phillips wrote one article entitled "The Madness of Great Wealth!" Of this, Russell wrote: "Few gave heed to the article, but it contained the heart and gist of the whole business. What on earth did a man want of a hundred million dollars any more than of a hundred million vest buttons that he should cheat and duck and lie and maneuver incessantly to wrest dollars from the grasp of need? Yet it was not really the dollar that made men mad; it was the trancing vision of the power that went with the dollar, and the men were not really so money crazed as they were touched with the old obsession of dominion—and kudos. What the Orient was to Tamburlaine, Wall Street was to Thomas Fortune Ryan."

This kind of thinking led Russell to embrace socialism, much to the horror of Phillips, who feared that Russell's

135

influence would be weakened. But it was not. Russell's integrity and prestige were so generally acknowledged that he went on writing, exposing and making a tremendous impact.

One of his most explosive endeavors focused on the horrible, disease-ridden tenements that returned an annual fortune to New York's historic Trinity Church. Trinity stands now as it did then on Broadway at the head of Wall Street. As the oldest church in New York, it owned outright large tracts of exceedingly valuable real estate. Its franchise had been approved by the English crown in 1697, and eight years later the church had been granted those sweeping acres that were to become whole blocks in the downtown section of the growing city. Land was cheap in those colonial days when New York was little more than a village, but as New York grew into a metropolis, with land ever more scarce and valuable, those holdings so casually granted became a source of great wealth.

The church early adopted the policy of leasing the land to those who wished to build upon it. In this fashion, merchants and other well-to-do persons constructed rows of two- and three-story brick and wood one-family homes. However, when their leases expired, Trinity often refused to renew them. The homeowner was then presented with a hard choice: he could tear his home down and cart away the bricks and lumber piece by piece—or he could walk away and leave the structure to Trinity. Thus, Trinity acquired entire blocks of such houses for little more than a song; and in the decades the church had owned the buildings, they had become rabbit warrens, several families packed into each one-family house, some of them immigrants, others native-born Americans struggling for a living at the very bottom of the economic scale.

This was the situation in 1908 when Charles Edward Russell turned his savage pen to an indictment of Trinity's role as a slum landlord. In April–May 1908 he wrote two articles for *Broadway Magazine* (later, *Hampton's*), a periodical destined to flourish longer than most of its muck-raking kin and to die a death that was to be a symbol and a warning to them all. This *Broadway* series was entitled "Trinity: Church of Mystery." Russell followed it up in *Everybody's,* in July 1908, with an article called "The Tenements of Trinity Church."

One catches the flavor of his style and its deadly impact is this last article in which he described the horrible tenements that cluttered Trinity's land on the West Side of New York from Broadway to the docks along the Hudson River. Listen:

"Drunken, disreputable, decayed, topsyturvy old houses, the homes of thousands of families and the breeding places of so many children that are to carry on the world's work— who owns these terrible places? Who draws the wretched profit of their existence?

"Trinity Church, holder of one of the greatest estates in New York or in the country, owns many of them. This is the heart of her possessions: street after street is lined with her properties . . ."

Russell detailed Trinity's tenement holdings, each enumeration thudding home like a series of blows struck in the prize ring: a dozen tenements on Clarkson Street; sixty-six on Varick; fifty-one on West Houston; sixty-five on Greenwich Street; twenty-six on Charlton Street; forty-seven on Canal Street; 138 on Hudson Street. His street

by street listing, exact in detail, deadly, built to a monu-
mental picture. "Wherever you walk in this dreadful region," he wrote, "you find something that Trinity owns,
and, as a rule, it is something that you know she ought
not to own."

The value of these miserable holdings had been estimated
at anywhere from $39,000,000 to $100,000,000, Russell wrote,
and no outsider could possibly determine the wealth Trinity
reaped from them. "For many years," he explained, "no
investigator has been able to obtain any more definite
knowledge of these matters than that this is the wealth of
Trinity which she holds for good purposes." What purposes?
he asked. Was this just Trinity's private business or did
it affect the entire community? He gave this answer:

"I have before me the testimony of a very eminent
authority about tenement houses, and she says that confirmed tenement house dwellers are as a class sickly, ane-
mic, lethargic, and show unmistakable tendencies toward
constitutional weakness. Tuberculosis has a strong hold
upon them; the effect of tenement house life is such that
the third generation of tenement house dwellers (if you
can conceive of a third generation) is usually of an in-
ferior mentality, without intelligent interest in anything,
leads dull and vacant lives, and furnishes recruits for the
reformatory and the state prison."

Russell found four or five families crowded into each
of these old one-family houses. He went into building after
building. He found in all of them only a single water tap
in the hallways on each of the floors. Originally, the houses
had had no water at all, but a tenement house law passed
a few years previously—legislation that Trinity had fought
furiously in the courts—had compelled the reluctant

churchly landlord to install these hallway water taps. The only sanitary facilities, however, remained wooden out-houses in the squalid backyards, a condition "one might expect to see in Chinese cities, but never in the foremost city of America."

Typical of these miserable hovels that bred crime and vice and disease was a Trinity tenement on Clarkson Street near Hudson. Russell gave this description:

"It presents to the street a dirty brick front, scaly, like its fellows, and long demanding paint . . . An old house, very old, very poorly built, very flimsy, very ramshackle. Everything about it seems to be going to decay. The halls are narrow, dark, dirty, and smell abominably. The stair-ways are narrow, wooden and insecure. On the second and third floors are interior bedrooms that have no natural light or ventilation, and must therefore, according to the Board of Health, be a prolific breeding place for the germs of tuberculosis . . ."

Even this sagging structure was almost a palace compared to some others that Russell visited.

"Come, then," he wrote, "into the filthy back yards at the rear of No. 20 Clarkson Street, and, looking over the rotting fences, you may discover a peculiarity of many of the houses in this region. The front walls are of brick; the rear and side walls are wooden. On the wooden walls the clapboards sag and sway and are falling off, the ancient laths and plaster are exposed beneath. Window panes are broken out. On one of the days when I was there, a bitter day in December, an icy wind blew through these apertures. I went into some of the living rooms. There were women and children around the fire in the one stove that cooked for them and gave them heat. They were trying to keep warm—with coal they bought by the pailful at the rate of $16 a ton. They paid $5.50 a month for the two miserable rooms—one with light, one without. [And this, it should be remembered, was in a day when the purchasing value of the dollar was worth many times what it is now.]"

These tenements were all fire traps, with no fire escapes. In some instances, a second house had been built on the rear of a single lot, and the only way of getting in and out of it was through a narrow wooden tunnel that connected it with the hallway of the house in front. If fire broke out, the inhabitants of such rear-lot dwellings would be trapped and incinerated in the flaming tunnel that was their only escape route.

"So runs this extraordinary story," Russell concluded. "Many strange features pertain to it. The managing forces of Trinity control a very great property. The real owners of that property are the communicants of the church. For ninety-four years, none of the owners has known the extent of the property, nor the amount of revenue therefrom, nor what is done with the money. The management is a self-perpetuating body, without responsibility and without supervision. All these are strange conditions. But stranger than all is this: that a Christian church should be willing to take money from such tenements as Trinity owns in the old Eighth Ward."

In introducing this exposé, the editors of *Everybody's* commented that Russell posed this "very great and interesting question: whether the good wrought by the charitable and philanthropic enterprises of Trinity equals the evil wrought by the tenements that finance the charities."

Russell's article, accompanied by photographs that verified the conditions he described, caused a sensation. The reaction was two-sided: on one level, a roar of outrage against Trinity; on higher and more influential levels, a roar of outrage against Russell. President Roosevelt had previously delivered his "muckraker" speech, attempting to discredit the journalists who were painting such unflattering views of American society. The counterattack by The Powers That Rule, in Josiah Flynt's phrase, was now well under way, and Russell's exposure of Trinity was denounced as a prime example of the extent to which these terrible journalists were prepared to go. Why, they were now attacking even the church!

In his autobiography years later, Russell wrote: "The series . . . started a cyclone of resentment, particularly in our highest social circles. The Reverend Morgan Dix, chief pastor of Trinity, died in the midst of the engagement and it was poignantly suggested that grief and chagrin over the attacks upon his corporation had caused his death." But, Russell added: "The smoke of the battle finally cleared away. Trinity had the usual vindication, the wickedness of the muckraker was satisfactorily demonstrated and all was once more peace. Then Trinity began quietly to tear down its objectionable tenements."

In the three years that followed the publication of Russell's exposé, Trinity destroyed scores of what Russell called "these filthy old barracks." The muckraker had been appropriately denounced and condemned by the "best" elements of society—but then he had been quietly and inconspicuously vindicated by the actions of his enemies who, in the deed, pleaded guilty to his charges.

The year 1908 was a busy one for Russell. Just one month before he attacked Trinity in *Everybody's*, he had set the entire state of Georgia on its ear by exposing the

incredible evils of a prison-farm system that leased convicts to private contractors, hard and brutal men who
used the lash and mistreated their human cattle just as
the worst of plantation overseers had done to Negro slaves
before the Civil War.

Russell's foray into Georgia was triggered by a letter
written to *Everybody's* by a former prisoner. The ex-convict
described such horrible conditions that *Everybody's* sent
Russell to Georgia to check up on his story and get a
description of the prison camps. The result was the article,
"A Burglar in the Making." In an introductory note, the
editor pointed out that Russell naturally could not disclose
the name of his informant, but he added that Russell himself had independently checked and verified many of the
facts. These, the editor wrote, "reveal clearly the shameful
system by which the State of Georgia surrenders for profits
the solemn duty of correcting her wrongdoers . . ."

Russell told the story of a young man whom he called
simply "George." George had embezzled $300 from the
till of his employer to play the horses; his penalty, four
years in prison. He was a thin and sickly youth, weighing
only 110 pounds, with valvular heart disease. But under
the system by which Georgia "sold" her convicts to private
employers for slave labor, George was shipped off with a
prison gang to a brick-making compound located in the
wilds of the state, where there was no supervision, no one
to stay the hands of brutal guards.

A high stockade with guard pens around it and men
with rifles handy occupied one corner of the dreary brick-
yard. Inside the stockade were "wretched, dark, dilapidated
and most filthy huts" in which the men were doomed to
sleep and eat. George saw at first glance that the workers

were "very badly clad, and some went almost naked." He and his fellow recruits were taken into one of the huts and given a breakfast of one slice of boiled salt pork and one piece of greasy corn bread. "There were no knives or forks, and George took the pork into his fingers. He felt something move under his fingers. He looked sharply at the pork. He saw what it was that moved. It was worms."

George was "amazed to see that the persons engaged in removing the bricks from the drying belts were women. He remembered then that the State of Georgia has no prison for convicted women, and that they are rented to slave brokers just as the men slaves are rented." George was given a wheelbarrow and told that he must wheel loads of bricks along a path four hundred feet long to the baking kilns. He was given a quota. He must deliver 105 of these 300 pound loads each day; if he failed to meet his quota, it would go hard with him.

He soon learned what "hard" meant. On this very first day, a frail convict, fifty-five years old, suffering from chronic rheumatism, lame, had been able to lug only fifty-seven loads instead of sixty by noontime. Because he was just three loads behind schedule, he was seized, stripped, spread-eagled across a barrel. Two Negroes held his arms and head; two others, his legs. An overseer loomed over him, in his hands a whip made of sole leather three inches wide, three feet long and three-eighths of an inch thick, with a stout wooden handle. Russell described the punishment in these words:

". . . The man lifts the instrument high in the air. He brings it down, *swish!* upon the naked man on the barrel. The man on the barrel screams aloud with sudden agony.

He does not shout or exclaim, he screams a horrible shrill scream of unutterable pain.

"The other man raises the instrument and brings it down, *swish!* again. Again the man on the barrel screams. A blow and a scream: a blow and a scream. Presently it is a blow and a sob: the man on the barrel is crying. Again a moment, and his blood trickles down his side; he is screaming, sobbing, crying now—and bleeding. The blows fall upon his bruised and bloody back; he wriggles and twists about; the Negroes can hardly hold down his head and his legs; the other men stand and gaze; the guards hold their rifles; and from the bluest of skies the soft sun of Georgia looks upon the frightful scene, and the sweet spring air from the southern woods blows over it."

This brutal scene was repeated again and again in the years George spent in the camp. "Three times in one day he saw that same old man whipped, the man that had rheumatism in his back: three times, and for no fault but failing to make the right number of loads." When one prisoner became so ill he could not work, some charitable society in a nearby town, happening to hear of his case, sent him special food and chickens to be made into broth; he never got the donation—the guards appropriated it. The shoes furnished the prisoners were made of such flimsy stuff they shredded away and the men walked, bare-toed, through the winter slush. But when friends of one prisoner sent him several pairs of socks and a new pair of shoes, all he got was one pair of socks—and he soon noticed that one of the guards was wearing socks just like his, and a fine new pair of shoes.

George, who had started his term hoping he might be able to atone for the $300 theft, to reform and redeem his life, came to the conclusion that this was a society without morals, without scruples—a society in which the strong, almost as a matter of principle, preyed on the weak. And so, once he had managed by some miracle to survive in this hell hole, "he went back to Atlanta and turned burglar."

No tornado striking suddenly across the Georgia flatlands could have caused a greater commotion than the publication of this exposé. The state legislature, its feathers fluttering in the gale, ordered an investigation. Hearings were held. And, to the horror of all Georgia, they established, not that Russell was some evil muckraker who had exaggerated unconscionably, but that on the contrary he was a careful reporter who, if anything, had understated the case. Take, for example, the bank of headlines, reflecting the disclosures at one day's hearing:

CONVICTS BEATEN TO DEATH,
SAY WITNESSES UNDER OATH
Revolting Stories of Cruelty at
Prison Camps Told In-
vestigating Committee
200 to 300 floggings
monthly at one camp,
testifies employee

One contractor admitted that he had pocketed between $200,000 and $300,000 in one five-year period through his "leasing" of convicts from the state. The evidence was overwhelming, irrefutable. All Georgia was shocked. The legislature, after much wrangling and indecision, passed legislation that would begin to reform a prison program that treated convicts like the slaves of old.

Such, then, was the work of Charles Edward Russell, and some of the things he managed to accomplish with

145

his trenchant pen. But this was not his only role, his only importance. He figured in a pivotal way, through no fault of his own, in a series of developments that were to crush muckraking and deny the muckrakers their outlets.

Russell's first contribution to the downfall of muckraking was a brilliant idea. He described how it came to him in these passages in his autobiography:

"One day early in 1905, I was sitting in the press gallery of the United States Senate observing the proceedings which were, as usual, languid. Directly in front of me on the floor below was a row of well-fed and portly gentlemen, every one of whom, we knew perfectly well, was there to represent some private (and predatory) Interest. Each was supposed to represent the people; each was in fact representing some division of the people's enemy. Looking over the rest of the Senate, I was struck with the patent fact that almost nobody in that chamber had any other reason to be there than his skill in valeting for some powerful Interest, and I thought a series of articles might well be written on the fact that strictly speaking we had no Senate; we had only a chamber of butlers for industrialists and financiers."

Fired up by the idea of taking on the members of the Senate one by one, devoting a full article to the misdeeds of each, Russell returned to New York and conferred with the editors of *Everybody's*. Now it was one thing to attack a soulless corporation; quite another to attack powerful men who presumably had souls. The corporation could hardly sue for the libeling of its character since it was not supposed to possess any, but individuals certainly could. The editors of *Everybody's* called in their lawyers, and these cautious gentlemen considered the dangers, shook their heads and pronounced the whole venture too risky.

Russell was not so easily dissuaded. His old mentor, William Randolph Hearst, had just bought control of a down-at-heels magazine, *Cosmopolitan*. Hearst brought in one of his top editors and began to transform *Cosmopolitan* into a top-grade muckraking magazine. Russell took his Senate-exposé idea to Hearst, who liked it instantly, and Russell had started his research when *Everybody's* came up with an assignment that entranced him. He was to go around the world and see how democracy worked in other nations. Russell abandoned the Senate project, and it was turned over to his friend, David Graham Phillips. And it was Phillips's blistering, devastating attack that ultimately was to put Teddy Roosevelt on the spot and lead to his muckraking speech in which he threw the prestige of the presidency against the crusading journalists. From that point on, the pressures to silence the critical voices that reverenced no one mounted almost day by day.

"Many of the magazine editors took fright at the presidential command and abandoned exposé stuff," Russell later wrote. "Others continued it, more or less timidly. There were other forces than any emanating from the White House, and more ruthless, to check the tide. Speaking at a Chamber of Commerce banquet in a Western town, the president of a New York City bank made the emphatic declaration that there would be no more muckraking in this country. In plain terms he declared that business had suffered all the attacks it intended to endure and that the slanderers of the leaders of the nation's commerce would be silenced."

In the event, they were. Russell himself was soon to

become a principal target of the silencers, and he was to have a tragic, inside view of the methods they could employ to bring down a fine magazine.

In 1907 Benjamin B. Hampton, a man of unusual principle and courage, bought *Broadway,* a struggling magazine with a mere 12,000 circulation. By spending money, employing some of the best writers of the day and featuring well-documented exposés, he built the circulation of the magazine that he renamed *Hampton's* to 480,000 in just three years. His success certainly indicated that, despite the Rooseveltian blast and business pressures, the public wanted more muckraking.

Russell, back from his world tour, began to write for *Hampton's.* He quickly found that he was a target of the repressionists, who assigned private detectives to dog his every footstep.

"For many weeks," he wrote, "I never left the hotel without being followed. At that time on the opposite side of the street stood a row of stables . . . There was one man that every evening snuggled himself into the disused entrance to one of these stables and watched for me. As soon as I came out I could see him over my shoulder stealthily moving in the wake. In those days the old Hoffman House was still standing. It had two entrances, one in Broadway and one in the side street. I would enter briskly at the Broadway side, come out on the side street and then again into Broadway where I would suddenly confront the sleuth to his manifest amazement and dismay. It is not altogether the happiest sensation in the world to feel that one is always under a slinking and malignant scrutiny, but in this case the annoyance was erased in amusement. The whole performance struck one as infinitely childish, preposterous, and laying bare the stupidity of what was called 'business acumen.' Nothing I had been able to say against entrenched respectability warranted that I should be dogged day and night . . ."

When Russell described this shadowing to a friend, the latter warned: "What they expect is to get you into a woman scrape. Watch your step, my son."

The woman trap failing, another device was now tried. Russell soon found a "swarm of agile-tongued prospectors" haunting his doorstep. All pointed out to him easy and infallible ways by which he could transform himself into a millionaire. One "persistent visitor from East Orange" insisted that Russell "could make $50,000 in a day by printing one statement in my next article and then buying or selling some stock." If Russell had fallen for any of these schemes, his integrity would have been destroyed; it would have been easy to expose and ruin him. But Russell was a man who could not be reached—and he went right on muckraking.

He now did a series of articles for *Hampton's* that was to ruin that gallant magazine, about the last true muckraking journal that was left. The series dealt with "the more conspicuous railroad scandals of America, the historic swindles by which one great fortune after another had been created at an enduring public expense." In due time, he got around to dealing with the record of the New Haven Railroad, and his article on the New Haven had been set in type and was in proof form when "a well-dressed and important-looking man" who said he represented the railroad called on Hampton.

It quickly became apparent to the publisher that his visitor, through the activity of some spy planted in *Hampton's* inner circle, knew everything that was in Russell's pending article. The article, said the visitor, was "a tissue of lies," it was libelous and malicious from beginning to end, there wasn't an accurate word in it—and he had come to demand that it be suppressed.

"Well," said Hampton, "we will not print in this magazine anything we know to be untrue. Here are the proofs of the article. Suppose we go over it and you point out the things that are untrue and if you can show that they are so we will omit them."

"It is all untrue," declared the visitor. "It is just one string of lies from beginning to end."

Hampton picked up the proofs and read the first sentence.

"Is that true or untrue?" he asked.

"Oh, well, of course, I don't mean that," said the visitor. "I mean when you get down into the heart of the thing."

"You said it was all untrue," Hampton reminded him. "We must read it all and see if you are right."

He then read the next sentence.

"Is that true or untrue?"

"Wait until you get past the introduction."

The reading went on, sentence by sentence, until finally Hampton came to the statement that in ten years the capital stock of the railroad had been increased by 1501 per cent—a process known as "watering."

"There," shouted the visitor, "that statement is a damn lie."

"Is it?" said Hampton.

He reached into the drawer of his desk and pulled out a copy of the *Congressional Record*, containing the explicit testimony to back up the assertion.

In this fashion, they went through the entire article; and the railroad emissary, who had said it was all a pack of lies, couldn't point out a single lie. But, he said, the article was "injurious to the railroad and we demand that it be suppressed."

"It will be printed," said Hampton.

"Then I must tell you that if you print that article your magazine will be put out of business. That is all."

With this warning, the visitor left. Hampton printed the article—and the visitor's threat quickly came true.

No matter how prosperous a magazine is, there are periods of the year, usually in summer, when revenue lags and financing is needed from the banks. With a flourishing magazine like *Hampton's,* there had never been any difficulty in getting this temporary financing; the magazine's overall revenues in a year were such that these borrowings had always been quickly paid off. Its credit was excellent. But now when Hampton went to a bank with which he had dealt for years and applied for his customary loan, he was refused. "The cashier was a friend of his," Russell wrote. "He [Hampton] asked for the reason of the refusal and was told confidentially that orders had come not to let *Hampton's* have any money."

Hampton had resources of his own, and he was a man not easily stopped. He got together a portfolio of his own gilt-edged securities and offered them at another bank as security for the loan he wanted. In such circumstances, with a loan fully guaranteed, it was unheard of that it should be refused. But in Hampton's case it was. "First and last," Russell wrote, "he offered that collateral to twenty-four banks and trust companies in New York and was refused by all." *Hampton's* was killed.

The muckrakers struggled on for another three years in a magazine known as *Pearson's.* But in the end the same

tactics were employed to kill off *Pearson's,* and the muckrakers no longer had a forum. "Muckraking in America
came to its death," Russell later wrote, "by strangulation
at the hands of persons and Interests perfectly well known.

"Doubtless Respectable Business was glad. Whether the
country had reason to rejoice is another question. Where
there is no criticism there is no health—in a democracy, at
least . . ."

CHAPTER VIII

David Graham Phillips

DAVID GRAHAM PHILLIPS was thirty-nine in 1906 when he took up Charles Edward Russell's suggestion that the members of the U. S. Senate should be exposed one by one.

Phillips was already famous, an arresting and challenging personality. Tall, strikingly handsome, always dressed in the best of taste, Phillips worked incredible hours, turned out astonishing quantities of colorful prose, and seemed well on his way to the realization of his dream of becoming the Balzac of American letters.

His working methods were novel. He had built for himself a high drafting table, scaled perfectly to his height so that he would not have to stoop; and before this he stood every night, seven nights a week, dashing off reams of longhand script. He began writing at ten o'clock in the evening, smoking innumerable cigarettes as he labored,

153

and worked straight through to dawn. Friends passing through New York's Gramercy Park in the small hours would look up at his lighted window, high up in the apartment house where he lived, and they would shake their heads. "There is Phillips pounding away at his high black pulpit," they would say.

By such prodigious labor, Phillips turned out between 6000 and 7000 words of finished copy a night. This Niagara of words produced two novels a year, supplemented by a stream of stories and muckraking magazine articles. Phillips once described the philosophy that drove him to such incessant labor in these words:

"Work, work, whether you want to or not. I throw away a whole day's work sometimes, but the effort of turning it out had kept my steam up and prevented me from lagging behind."

Phillips, like his friend, Russell—like so many of the other muckrakers—was a Midwesterner with the deeply inbred ideals of an individualistic society not many removes from the frontier. He was born in Madison, Indiana, in 1867. The town, fifty miles above Louisville on the Ohio River, had been settled only sixty-one years before. It was for a time the wealthiest city in the new state, a key port for steamboat traffic; but, with the development of the railroads, river commerce became less important and Madison went into eclipse.

Phillips's father, an Indiana farm boy, had risen to become cashier of the Madison National Bank, sheriff and clerk of the court. He was a stanch Republican, and Phillips grew up in a middle-class, conservative atmosphere compounded of banking, Republican politics, daily Bible readings and Methodist morality. In his home, there was one

other element, an important one—a love of books and literature. His father possessed one of the best private libraries in
southern Indiana, and the boy early became an avid reader
of books.

After finishing public school, he went to what is now
DePauw University, where his roommate, a boy from a less
advantaged family, was the hard-working, brilliant Albert
Beveridge—in later life a U. S. Senator, a leading Progressive, and Phillips's steadfast friend. In 1885 Phillips transferred to Princeton University, where he became a colorful
figure on the campus, noted as a brilliant conversationalist
and a fastidious dresser.

It was while he was at Princeton that Phillips charted
the course of his life. He was determined to become a
famous novelist; but, first, he decided, he must see life
whole, just as it was—and so he would become a reporter.
When he graduated from Princeton in 1887, a family friend
got him a job as a reporter on the Cincinnati *Times-Star*.
After serving a three-year apprenticeship there, he moved
to New York in 1890 and went to work for the New York
Sun, which had one of the best newspaper staffs of the day.

He soon settled into what was to become for him a life
pattern. He dressed extremely well, in the high-collared
fashion of the day. He lived in tasteful bachelor's quarters,
either at the Players, a private club for actors and writers
in Gramercy Park, or in one of the apartment houses
nearby. He dined in Delmonico's and other equally famous
restaurants. He worked until late at night at the *Sun* and
then returned to his quarters, and wrote until dawn on
stories and articles. In 1891 *Harper's Weekly* published the
first of these articles written in his off-duty time—and the
flood gates were open.

Phillips soon left the *Sun* and joined its famous rival, the *World*. Here he rose swiftly. The *World* sent him to London as a foreign correspondent; and, upon his return after the tour abroad, he became an editorial writer and then the private secretary to the publisher, Joseph Pulitzer. The publisher, one of the most famous in the history of American journalism, was then slowly going blind; and he liked to have this colorful young man around him, engaging Phillips in many long private conversations and attempting to shape his ideals, as a father might those of a son.

The *World* was the leading Democratic newspaper in the nation, but it was noted above all for a crusading spirit that pulled no punches, regardless of party or creed. It was concerned in the 1890s, during the presidency of Grover Cleveland, a Democrat, about the growing, enormous power of the trusts and their increasing dominance of American life. Though the Sherman Anti-Trust Act was on the law books, though Cleveland had taken office making trust-busting noises, nothing had been done to fulfill his campaign pledges to the people. Pulitzer assigned Phillips to the task of writing a series of articles attacking the Cleveland administration, reciting the sins of the trusts and calling for action. In article after article, Phillips blasted away, presenting a scorching indictment of business misdeeds and calling on Cleveland's Attorney General, Richard Olney, to curb the trusts. The citizens of the nation, Phillips thundered, had been betrayed by false promises, and he closed every article with the same line: "Such, Mr. Olney, are the facts, and here, sir, is the law," following this with a quotation of the provisions of the Sherman Act. Phillips, though he could not know it at the time, was honing the weapons he would later use in his explosive "The Treason of the Senate."

This first heavy journalistic barrage in the *World,* however, had little effect. The business-dominated Cleveland administration could not be prodded into bestirring itself; and so, shortly after the turn of the century, having served a fourteen-year apprenticeship in journalism, Phillips decided to cut loose and pursue his real goal, writing fiction that would depict the realities of his time as he saw them. His decision was made easier by the attention attracted by his first novel, *The Great God Success,* published in 1901.

It was a story that was a bitter account of life in the newspaper world, and it drew heavily, as first novels so often do, on many of Phillips's personal experiences. The book attracted the attention of George Horace Lorimer, then the editor of *The Saturday Evening Post,* and Lorimer persuaded Phillips to leave the newspaper business and write full time. Phillips did; and, in the next three years, he produced some fifty signed articles and editorials for Lorimer, including political portraits of Roosevelt, Cleveland, Rockefeller, and the banking czar, J. P. Morgan. During the same period, his articles and short stories flooded such magazines as *Everybody's, Cosmopolitan, Harper's, McClure's, The Arena* and *Collier's.*

In this prodigious magazine production and in the novels that flowed from his pen, Phillips held to one fixed purpose and made his philosophy clear. His aim, which he pursued with an almost fanatical intensity, was truth, and he insisted on seeing truth whole, with no compromises, however unpalatable and ugly it might be. "I have no mission, no purpose, no cult," he said once; "I am a novelist, telling as accurately as I can what I see and trying to hold my job with my readers."

Phillips's whole-truth fixation daunted even some of his friends who were notable truth-seekers themselves. Charles Edward Russell, certainly a man of integrity and unblinking courage, was one who found that Phillips's mania for truth exceeded even his own. They had many discussions about this, and Russell later wrote:

"I used to try to point out to him that occasions arise in which it is needful for even the best of men to compromise with the bald truth, but he would never admit this . . . He and I were at Carlsbad one season and walked about the streets and hillpaths discussing this with one invariable result. 'Well, I don't see how you can say so,' says Graham."

Like Russell, Phillips saw the problems of the time through Midwestern eyes. His was the viewpoint of the free and independent men, the fiercely individualistic men, who had stood sturdily on the land of their own quarter sections, who believed that one man was just as good as another, who had a passionate faith in one-to-one democracy and an equally passionate distrust of anything smacking of aristocracy and concentrated wealth. They distrusted the East with its mounting money power and its high-living society that aped the fashions of Europe and considered it a coup to marry off a rich daughter to an impoverished foreign title. Viewing this scene with his reporter's clear-eyed perception and his Midwestern faith, Phillips wrote in the pitiless, challenging vein that quickly attracted attention and a popular following.

The chord was struck in his first novel, *The Great God Success*. In it, Phillips had his principal character remark: "Freedom's battles are never won by men with full stomachs and full purses." And again: "I wonder, he replied slowly, does a rich man own his property or does it own him?"

In another of his early books, *The Reign of Gilt*, published in 1905, Phillips wrote: "It is as exact a truth as any in chemistry or mechanics that Aristocracy is the natural, the inevitable sequence of widespread ignorance, and Democracy the natural, inevitable sequence of widespread intelligence . . . Because of these spectacles of sloth, incompetence, and corruption in public officials, it is charged by many persons of reputation as 'Publicists' that Democracy is a breeder of corruption. The truth is just the reverse. Democracy drags public corruption out of its mole tunnel where it undermines society, drags it into the full light of day . . ."

The heritage of the old Midwestern frontier showed in Phillips's attitude toward inherited wealth and society, themes that recur again and again in his fiction. He drew devastating pictures of idle dowagers who sat upon their departed husbands' money bags and of the so-called "society" and "culture" that resulted. This "culture," he wrote acidly, represented a fine flowering into nothing; it had all the quality of "a fog bank."

In *The Second Generation*, published in 1907, Phillips built his plot around the theme "shirt-sleeves to shirt-sleeves in three generations." The first generation was represented, of course, by the hard-working go-getter who built the family fortune; the second, by his idle and worthless heirs who wasted it in those high-flinging "society" pursuits for which Phillips had only contempt; and the third generation was back in shirt-sleeves, virtually at the same low point at which the family saga had started.

"It is the curse of the world, this inherited wealth . . ."

Phillips wrote. "Because of it society moves in circles instead of forward. The ground gained by the toiling generations is lost by the inheriting generations. And this accursed inheritance tempts men ever to long for and hope for that which they have not earned."

In this novel, one of Phillips's most appealing characters comes to a tragic and unnecessary end at the hands of a murdering madman—a fictional episode almost identical with the one that was to cut prematurely short the career of Phillips himself.

The views that Phillips expressed in his writings gave him all the coloration of a radical to the conservatives of his time. He was, perhaps, a radical—but an individualistic radical. As has been noted, he opposed Russell's advocacy of socialism, and he himself never tied himself to any clique, party, or movement. As Mrs. Anna S. Walling, who knew him well, later wrote in *The Saturday Evening Post*, "he was always himself, with a program of his own . . . he in all his work had one aim—to unmask his time and pursue it to the bitter end."

Such was the man who was given the task of carrying out Russell's idea for an exposé of the Senate. When Russell left on his world tour, Bailey Millard, Hearst's editor on *Cosmopolitan*, turned at once to Phillips. But Phillips was cold to the whole idea.

His novels had become best-sellers, and he felt that he had now reached the point in his career at which he could abandon magazine work and devote himself completely to his fiction. He suggested that Millard get William Allen White to write the Senate series. White, however, didn't want to undertake it, and Millard returned again and again to Phillips.

Having come to know Phillips well, Millard put pressure on him at his weakest and most sensitive point. He appealed to Phillips's social conscience; it was Phillips's duty, Millard said, to devote himself to a task of such importance. No one else could do it so well. Finally, Phillips consented.

Hearst gave him research help. Gustavus Myers, a sound historical researcher who had written a history of great American fortunes, and Phillips's brother, Harrison, a Denver newspaperman, were hired to gather material, though Phillips supplemented their efforts. Once committed, he plunged into the task as he always did with whatever he undertook—completely. Shelving all his other work, he went to Washington and personally scouted the Senate scene. It was well that he did, for Millard later disclosed that some of the most devastating anecdotes in the series were obtained by Phillips himself from Senators disgusted with the system.

Having gathered his material, Phillips launched into the writing of the series with all the outraged fury and passion that marked his style. Night after night, he stood at his "high black pulpit," writing on pads of yellow, lined paper the words that were to scar mighty members of the Senate and to stir up a tempest in the nation rivaled only by the reaction to Upton Sinclair's *The Jungle*.

William Randolph Hearst, the supreme showman of journalism, kept a close eye on the developing series and launched it with a publicity campaign that whetted the curiosity of the nation. In a personal message to his readers in *Cosmopolitan*'s February 1906 issue, Hearst described the sensational series that was to begin in March and promised that its revelations would be so damaging Senators might have to resign. At the same time, placards proclaiming in huge type TREASON OF THE SENATE appeared on newsstands all over Washington.

The announcement came at a sensitive time. President Roosevelt had opened the first session of the 59th Congress by calling for railroad rate reforms, passage of the Pure Food and Drug Act, statehood for Oklahoma, an employers' liability act and a meat inspection bill. All of these measures were stalled in committees, especially in the Senate where servants of "the interests," as Phillips called them, held life and death power over legislation. Fierce debates over the proposed Hepburn railroad bill, which would have prevented the kind of scandalous rebates that had built Standard Oil, were raging at the very moment that Hearst's placards shouted "Treason."

Requests to reprint Phillips's series, sight unseen, flooded *Cosmopolitan*'s office in advance of the event. Newspapers in the West, where railroad chicanery was an especially volatile issue, were more than eager to obtain the reprint rights. This atmosphere of mounting national tension and interest assured the success of the series even before it appeared; and when the March 1906 issue of *Cosmopolitan* came out in mid-February, the supplies were swept off the stands almost as soon as they were delivered. Requests for more magazines and a flood of subscriptions poured into *Cosmopolitan*. No muckraking magazine, except perhaps *Everybody's* in the early days, had ever scored a success like it.

Cosmopolitan topped Phillips's first article with a bannered quotation from the Constitution:

"Treason against the United States shall consist only in levying war against them, *or in adhering to their enemies, giving them aid and comfort."*

By putting special emphasis on those last words, Hearst attempted to justify the title, "Treason of the Senate." Phillips carried out the theme in every article of the series, accusing the twenty-one Senators he profiled of being traitors to their country. To many, however, the use of the word "treason" appeared like the worst exaggeration of yellow journalism. There could be no doubt that the Constitutional definition concerned the betrayal of the nation to active foreign enemies; it had not been intended to apply to domestic policies, however mistaken or venal or vicious. But Hearst and Phillips equated the authors of such policies with treason, arguing that they had betrayed the people for the benefit of selfish interests.

One gets the spirit of the flaming attack from the very first sentence of Phillips's first article. He wrote:

"One morning during this session of Congress, the Senate blundered into a discussion of two of its minor disreputables, Burton and Mitchell, who had been caught with their fingers sliding about in the change pocket of the people."

The debate, he wrote, had concluded with Senator Henry Cabot Lodge, the Massachusetts Republican with the famous name, telling the Senate haughtily:

"There is too much tendency to remember the Senators and to forget the Senate."

Phillips hopped on this quotation, writing:

"Let us take Mr. Lodge's hint. Let us disregard the Senators as individuals; let us for a moment 'remember the Senate.' The treason of the Senate!"

He justified use of the term with an admission that turned into flaming denunciation in this manner:

"Treason is a strong word, but not too strong, rather too

weak, to characterize the situation in which the Senate is the eager, resourceful, indefatigable agent of interests as hostile to the American people as any invading army could be and vastly more dangerous; interests that manipulate the prosperity produced by all, so that it heaps up riches for the few; interests whose growth and power can only mean the degradation of the people, of the educated into sycophants, of the masses toward serfdom."

Phillips first article stripped bare the careers of the two Senators from President Roosevelt's home state of New York—Thomas Collier Platt, the Republican boss of the state, and Chauncey M. Depew. Platt, Phillips wrote, "had been caught stealing trust funds," and now this trust-fund thief was so senile he had actually wept tears of frustration on the Senate floor when President Roosevelt had refused to name a U. S. Attorney of his choice. Platt, Phillips wrote, treated Depew, who had been talking about retiring, with the contempt one holds for a jellyfish, browbeating Depew in the hearing of other Senators and telling him he would do what Platt told him to do and retire when Platt told him to retire. Phillips pictured Depew as a man who had possessed assets of charm and ability in the beginning, but who had quickly sold out to the highest bidders—"the interests." By this sellout, Depew had become a member of the boards of directors of seventy corporations, receiving more than $50,000 annually in fees for his services—and, naturally, he protected the interest of "the interests" he represented in the Senate. Of Platt, Phillips wrote that he had a "long . . . unbroken record of treachery to the people in legislation of privilege and plunder promoted and in decent legislation prevented."

This was a theme—privilege and plunder on the one

hand; decent legislation pigeonholed on the other—that Phillips was to develop with even more savage effect in his second article in the series. He focused in this on the career of Nelson W. Aldrich, the senior Senator from Rhode Island, whom he described as the boss of the Senate. Phillips was to be much berated by his critics for his use of denunciatory adjectives and adverbs—and a paucity of facts. The adjectives and adverbs were certainly extreme, but facts were there, too. This was probably never better illustrated than in Phillips's treatment of Aldrich.

In describing Aldrich's power and the basis for it, Phillips bore down heavily on an issue that was to assume great importance. He emphasized that Senators were being selected by a closed tight little circle of bosses, the members of the Senates in the individual states; the people did not vote for them, the people had no say. What this meant, Phillips explained, was that "the interests," if they could bribe or pressure a majority of a state Senate, could name their own hand-picked agents to sit in the powerful Senate of the United States, where they were appointed to important committees and where they worked their will on legislation, killing bills that might have hurt "the interests," seeing measures were passed that lined private pockets with literally millions of dollars extorted from the people.

Rhode Island was a marvelous illustration of the way in which this restricted selection of Senators benefited the small circle of their private backers. The state constitution provided that each city and township should be considered a political unit, with equal weight in the state Senate. As a result, Rhode Island's five cities, where two-thirds of the population lived, were swamped by the voting strength of twenty "almost vacant rural townships," where only 37,000

165

persons lived. Thus, Phillips wrote, "one-eleventh of the population, and they the most ignorant and most venal, elect a majority of the legislature—which means that they elect the two United States Senators."

Aldrich, who had been born in 1841, had begun his career as a grocery boy, had become a clerk in a fish store, had graduated to grocery bookkeeper, had then established a wholesale grocery business—and finally had entered politics. He had won the favor of the Republican boss, had proved himself a faithful servant of Rhode Island interests, had invested and made a fortune in utility franchises that, of course, had to be approved by the legislature in which he sat; and, as a reward for all this, he had been promoted to the U. S. Senate in 1881. In 1901 he had ratified his close ties to "the interests" when his only daughter married the only son of John D. Rockefeller. "Thus," Phillips wrote, "the chief exploiter of the American people [Rockefeller] is closely allied by marriage to the chief schemer in the service of their exploiters."

Returned to the Senate again and again by the closed political boss system of Rhode Island, with its strength founded in rural rotten boroughs, Aldrich had grasped such power that he was either the chairman or the dominating member of the most vital committees of the Senate. He blocked legislation the wealthy and powerful didn't want. And he saw to it that ever higher protective tariffs—tariffs that defied all reason and victimized the American people—were enacted to pour ever more millions of dollars into the hands of the chosen few. Phillips's Midwestern partiality to the little fellow showed in the rage with which he wrote that the Senate, under Aldrich's thumb, "has so legislated and so refrained from legislating that more than half of all the wealth created by the American people belongs to less than 1 per cent of them; that the income of the average American family has sunk to less than six hundred dollars a year; that of our more than twenty-seven million children of school age, less than twelve millions go to school, and more than two millions work in mines, shops, and factories."

Phillips wrote acidly of an occasion on which Aldrich's secret maneuvers on behalf of the interests had been exposed to the light of day. Much of the work of Congress, now as then, is done in committees, and committee actions are secret. All one usually knows is that a proposed bill had been approved or disapproved in committee; but the identity of the legislator who has altered a bill, or helped to kill it, is usually hidden behind the wall of committee secrecy. Phillips wrote that this protective system had broken down once in Aldrich's case because a fellow Senator, "angered by some misrepresentation made by Aldrich, had part of the minutes of a meeting of the finance committee read in open Senate—a gross breach of 'senatorial courtesy!' Before the rudely lifted curtain was dropped, the country had a rare, illuminatory view of Aldrich. Here is this official minute:

"'At a meeting of the Committee on Finance on March 17, 1894, on motion of Mr. Aldrich, the committee proceeded to a consideration of the provisions (of the Wilson Bill) in regard to an income tax. Mr. Aldrich moved that the whole provision be stricken out of the bill.'"

The disclosure, Phillips wrote, left Aldrich and another Senator who had always posed as a friend of "the plain people," flustered and red-faced. "It is the only time," he added, "the people have ever had a look at Aldrich in his

167

shirt sleeves and hard at his repulsive but remunerative trade."

Just as Aldrich had protected his wealthy backers from the pain of having to pay income taxes, so did he see to it that tariff schedules were written sky-high to guarantee them ever more enormous profits. Phillips traced the course of three different tariff bills. The pattern was always the same. The bills would originate in the House of Representatives, as all revenue measures must. In their original form they always adequately protected—even more than protected—American manufacturers against foreign competition. The measures would be passed by the House and sent to the Senate. There Aldrich's finance committee would take over, and there the tariff rates would be raised higher and higher until they became so high that the Congressman who had drafted the original bill felt positively disgraced to have his name connected with it.

The result was that the American consumer was being gouged through the higher prices he had to pay. The House of Representatives, whose members were elected directly by the people, sensed the mood of the electorate and tried at times to show what was happening. But Aldrich always defied them, throwing up every roadblock his power could devise to disguise the truth. Phillips wrote:

"When Bacon, in 1903, moved to call on the Department of Commerce and Labor for full facts about the selling of American goods at prices from one-fourth to a full hundred per cent cheaper abroad than at home, Aldrich at once moved to refer the resolution to his committee, and his motion was carried. A year later, Bacon reminded the Senate of his former resolution and of how it was sleeping in Aldrich's committee, and reintroduced it. He backed it up with masses of facts—how 'our' sewing machines sell abroad for fifteen dollars and here for twenty-five dollars; how 'our' borax, a Rockefeller product, costs seven and a half cents a pound here and only two and a half cents abroad; how 'our' nails, a Rockefeller-Morgan product, sell here for four dollars and fifty cents a keg and abroad for three dollars and ten cents; how the foreigner gets for one dollar as much of 'our' window glass as we get for two dollars . . . how the beef trust sold meat from twenty-five to fifty per cent dearer in Buffalo than just across the Canadian line; how the harvester trust sold its reapers cheaper on the continent of Europe than to an Illinois farmer coming to its main factory in Chicago; how on every article in common use among the American people of city, town and country, 'the interests' were boldly robbing the people.

"And Mr. Aldrich said, 'Absurd!' And the Senate refused even to call upon the Department of Labor for the facts."

Finishing off Aldrich, Phillips wrote:

"Has Aldrich intellect? Perhaps. But he does not show it. He has never in his twenty-five years of service in the Senate introduced or advocated a measure that shows any conception of life above what might be expected in a Hungry Joe. No, intellect is not characteristic of Aldrich— or of any of these traitors, or of the men they serve. A scurvy lot, are they not, with their smirking and cringing and voluble palaver about God and patriotism and their eager offerings of endowments for hospitals and colleges whenever the American people so much as looks hard in their direction!"

This "Aldrich treatment" was typical of the exposure, scorn and abuse to which Phillips subjected the twenty-one members of the Senate whom he attacked. He called Arthur Pye Gorman of Maryland, the Democratic Minority Leader, Aldrich's counterpart, "a grafter." He compared Joseph W. Bailey, a powerful Texas Democrat, to Judas Iscariot. He called Lodge the end product of a Massachusetts legislature devoted to public plunder and betrayal, wrote that this corrupted legislature had three times returned Lodge to Washington, and commented: "A stream can rise no higher than its source—that is not an axiom of physics only." He attacked Philander Chase Knox, who had been Roosevelt's Attorney General and had become a Republican Senator from Pennsylvania, as a man who had made millions "from armorplate and rebate rascals."

For nine months, Phillips kept up the barrage; and, as article followed article, Teddy Roosevelt's temper frayed. The President had many reasons for fury and for fear. Some of the Senators whom Phillips attacked were close to Roosevelt personally. Lodge was one; Knox, another. Then there were political considerations. Hearst, the publisher of *Cosmopolitan*, was a Democrat and Roosevelt's sworn enemy in New York; the "treason" series attacked eighteen Republicans and only three Democrats; and Roosevelt had reason to fear public reaction might doom his party and cost it control of Congress. In addition, there was the Roosevelt legislative program, all of it tied up in those Senate committees whose devious maneuvers Phillips had so graphically described. The pressures all combined to make Roosevelt deliver his famous speech, denouncing and deriding the muckrakers.

The presidential assault was the signal for a general attack on Phillips. He received threats against his life, and "the reactionary press," as Russell wrote, "rang with his name as chief among the sinners, while the President was everywhere praised for rebuking the slanderers of the upright and the good." Ellery Sedgwick was so shocked by the vehemence of Phillips's indictment of the Senate that he cried in alarm: "These men want Socialism!" And *Collier's*, which had done its own share of muckraking and had published Phillips's stories and articles, turned on him in an attack that hurt most of all. *Collier's* proclaimed that his "treason" series had "made reform odious" and added that the articles were "one shriek of accusations based on the distortion of such facts as were printed, and on the suppression of facts which were essential"—a statement that, in itself, was far more distorted than anything Phillips had ever written.

The voices that came to Phillips's defense—and there were several—were drowned out in the chorus of hostile criticism. Senator Albert J. Beveridge, his old friend from college days and a man certainly in a position to know many Senate secrets, congratulated him on the accuracy of the series. Immediately after Roosevelt delivered his muckraker speech, the New York *World* and the New York *Post* suggested that the President himself should be called a muckraker; for, said they, some of the most telling anecdotes Phillips had printed, items that the President didn't like to see in print, had originated right at his own White House dinner table. Roosevelt's sulphurous denunciations of members of the corrupted Senate were well known to Washington correspondents, and Lincoln Steffens and Upton Sinclair were only two among many who had heard the President hold forth in language that matched, if indeed it did not surpass, anything that Phillips had written.

All of this was little consolation to Phillips at the time.

He became convinced that he had failed miserably in his "Treason of the Senate" series. Russell later recalled how, after *Collier's* savage attack, "I had an anxious time with him that Sunday, walking him around the streets while I tried to comfort and console him under the blow." But Phillips was not to be cheered. He continued to regard "his series as the one failure of his career."

Oddly enough, Roosevelt himself, having loosed the hounds on Phillips, decided like a typical politician that there should be no personal animosity. He wanted to meet with Phillips personally to assure him of this; and three times he sent emissaries to the writer, trying to arrange a meeting. Three times, Phillips, hurt and scornful, refused even to see the President. Roosevelt persisted, however, and so the two finally met. Phillips found Roosevelt a fascinating character, but one for whom he had little respect. Phillips was a no-compromise idealist; Roosevelt, a practical politician skilled in the art of compromise to get things done—and, between the two, there could never be any close rapport.

Despite Roosevelt's muckraker blast, despite the attacks on Phillips in a press largely wedded to "the interests," it gradually became apparent that Phillips had scored heavily in his "treason" series. For one thing, there were no libel suits. Even Phillips's fiery language in excoriating some of the most powerful politicians in the nation did not lure any of them into the mistake of defending their honor in the courts. They were doubtless wise; for, though Phillips himself did not know it at the time, Hearst had begun as early as 1904 to purchase the dynamite-laden Archbold letters with their documentation of the manner in which Standard Oil bribed Senators in wholesale lots. Hearst continued buying and amassing this secret hoard until 1908, when he published another series that created a national furor.

More immediately apparent was the effect that Phillips's series had on the Senate itself. The public reaction to his disclosures had been widespread indignation. The Senate felt the heat. And suddenly Roosevelt's reform legislation, stalled so long in committees, began to find its way into the light from the darkness of those secret chambers. The Pure Food and Drug Bill came out of committee and was passed by a 63 to 4 Senate vote—the first Roosevelt reform measure, as some editorialists noted, to "run the gauntlet" of the Upper House. A battered and largely discredited Senate was in no position to throw roadblocks, and other Roosevelt measures—the Hepburn Bill regulating the railroads and Senator Beveridge's meat inspection amendment, which Roosevelt backed—came out of committees and whipped through Congress under the pressure of a public opinion even the Senators felt they could not defy. As Lincoln Steffens told Roosevelt to his face, he had cost himself the best support he had when he denounced the muckrakers, for they were the ones who were arousing the people by their disclosures and building support for the kind of progressive legislation Roosevelt wanted—and that his enemies in the Senate had so persistently blocked.

Such were the immediate and visible results of Phillips's series. There were other and longer-lasting effects.

Phillips's disclosures of senatorial rascality furnished ammunition for progressive and reform forces. "The Treason of the Senate" became the bible in many a political campaign. Some of the Senators whom Phillips had exposed didn't even dare to seek office again; others were defeated. By 1912, just six years later, the entire complexion of the

173

Senate had changed, and only four of the twenty-one Senators Phillips had profiled still retained their seats. And this was not all.

A nationwide movement gathered force for the popular election of Senators. The aim was to make as certain as possible that never again could a rural "rotten borough" system like that in Rhode Island give a few interests and their political mouthpieces the power to create a czar of the Senate. The Seventeenth Amendment calling for the popular election of Senators was introduced in Congress; and in the debates that raged in April 1911 many speeches rang with phrases lifted straight out of Phillips's articles.

Before this amendment—the crowning testament to Phillips's work—could be passed by Congress and adopted by the states, however, Phillips himself was dead. On January 24, 1911, a young musician, Fitzhugh C. Goldsborough, a member of an old and prominent Washington family, cornered Phillips and shot him six times. Goldsborough, it developed, had become deranged, obsessed with the mistaken idea that his sister had been persecuted by Phillips because one of Phillips's acidly drawn female fictional characters so greatly resembled her.

Phillips struggled for life through twenty-four agonized hours. Friends clustered around his bedside—among them Senator Beveridge, George Horace Lorimer, and Arthur Brisbane, the famous editorialist and columnist of the Hearst newspapers. Just before he lost consciousness for the last time, Phillips gasped:

"I could have won out against two bullets, but it is pretty hard against six."

He died, then, not realizing the extent of what he had accomplished. He died still believing that his greatest success had been his greatest failure. Though more than four years had passed since he finished "The Treason of the Senate," the articles, alone among the major muckraking performances of their time, had not found publication in book form. Publishers ran scared, and so the series lived only in the old back files of *Cosmopolitan*. It was not until 1964 that the articles were resurrected and finally published in book form by Quadrangle Books in Chicago.

Phillips's greatest success as a novelist also came years after his death. He had been working on his masterwork, *Susan Lenox: Her Fall and Rise*, the story of a prostitute. The manuscript was virtually finished when Phillips was murdered, and it was published in serial form in *Hearst's Magazine* from 1915 to 1917. Subsequently issued in book form, it sold hundreds of thousands of copies and became the most famous novel Phillips had written.

Deprived of the satisfaction that should have been his when a murdering madman cut short his career, David Graham Phillips nevertheless had performed the climactic feat of the muckraking age. Professor Louis Filler, the modern authority on the muckrakers, has written that Phillips's "The Treason of the Senate" marked "the high point of muckraking in its exposure phase." Attacked, villified, scorned though he was—even his novels treated with contempt by servile critics currying favor with the powerful in society—David Graham Phillips had perhaps scored the greatest success of all the muckrakers. He had been largely responsible for changing in one vital respect the Constitution of the United States.

CHAPTER IX

The End of an Era

BEFORE IT WAS strangled by financial powers that did not like muckraking, *Hampton's Magazine* ran a prophetic cover. It depicted huge iron chains, fastened by a lock labeled "Press Censor." Above one link of the chain appeared a question mark and below it these queries: "Will the Magazines Remain Free? Will They Withstand the Attacks of Wall Street and Big Politics?"

The answer to those questions, unfortunately for the American public, was "No." *Hampton's* died, and most of the other muckraking magazines died with it. S. S. McClure, who had started the vogue with the exposés of Lincoln Steffens and Ida Tarbell, lost control of *McClure's*. Upton Sinclair always claimed that "the interests" got *McClure's* just as they had *Hampton's*. McClure himself disputed this, arguing that his own "bad business methods" had run him into debt and given the West Virginia Pulp & Paper Company the chance to seize control of the magazine.

It seemed significant to almost everyone else, however, that McClure himself was put on the shelf at the remarkably early age of fifty-five. Here was a vital, vigorous man who had built McClure's syndicate and the magazine by a display of incredible energy, vision and guts in the best free-enterprise tradition; here was a man who was generally acknowledged to be the foremost editor of his day— but the instant business interests obtained control of his magazine, he was finished as an editor. Muckraking was dead in *McClure's*, and before long the magazine was dead, too.

As Charles Edward Russell wrote, the muckraking continued for a few short years, from 1912 to 1916, in the little-known *Pearson's*. Arthur West Little, who published *Pearson's*, was a friend of Russell and David Graham Phillips, and he felt that the muckrakers should have a forum. In his April 1912 issue he announced that he was determined to oppose the reactionary forces that were crippling the muckraking magazines. He took over the subscription list of *Hampton's* and began to publish articles by Russell and some of the other surviving muckrakers. Knowing he must be free from dependence on advertising, Little published *Pearson's* on cheap pulp paper and without any of the costly illustrations and entertainment features that had helped attract attention to *McClure's*. *Pearson's* would appeal to the public on the basis of contents only, Little announced, and, despite its unattractive format, it did.

The considerable following it attracted seemed to indicate that the public wanted more, not less, muckraking, but in the end *Pearson's* was killed just as *Hampton's* had been before it. And the healthy ferment and dissent the muckrakers had stirred up in the nation was replaced by blandness.

Many of the old muckraking magazines survived. *Collier's, Cosmopolitan, The American Magazine, Everybody's* (which had been transformed into a thing called *Romance Magazine*) made their regular appearances on the newsstands, but the old muckrakers who had made them famous would never have recognized them. For they challenged nothing. They aimed only to entertain; they became vehicles for pap.

The effect on the soul of the nation was profound. It can hardly be considered an accident that the heyday of the muckrakers coincided with one of America's most yeasty and vigorous periods of ferment. The people of the country were aroused by the corruptions and wrongs of the age—and it was the muckrakers who informed and aroused them. The results showed in the great wave of progressivism and reform cresting in the remarkable spate of legislation that marked the first administration of Woodrow Wilson from 1913 to 1917. For this, the muckrakers had paved the way.

A brief summary of some of the evils they had attacked and the reforms that followed shows just how much they accomplished. They had forced the breakup of Standard Oil and brought on an era of trust-busting, holding back for a time the creeping bigness of business combines that threatened to crush the spirit of free initiative in American life. They had exposed the meat-packing industry and had compelled reforms to protect the health of the American people. They had repeatedly attacked the czar-like powers of the railroad barons; and, in the end, even a bribed and corrupted Congress had had to yield to the public out-cry—had had to curb these mighty autocrats. They had exposed the evils of child labor; and in time legislation would be passed banning the employment of millions of small children in sweatshop factories and dangerous mines. They had brought about the popular election of United States Senators. In so many ways had they affected the currents of their time.

When their markets were closed to them, when the magazines that had given them a forum were put out of business, all America was the loser. The vogue of blandness and entertainment—the boy-meets-girl fiction and light articles that came to dominate the nation's magazines—coincided with eras of conformity and stagnation. Sloth and indifference marked the decade of the 1920s as business administrations in Washington promoted the excesses that would plunge the nation into the debacle of the Great Depression. The stock market went wild with gambling fever—and was unsupervised, unchecked. The protective tariff was raised to such prohibitive levels that all world trade was crippled, and disaster followed. Through it all, as the nation plunged blindly toward the abyss, there was little more than a murmur of criticism and dissent.

Some of the old muckrakers were still around, but they were no longer plying their trade. Ida Tarbell and Russell turned to the writing of biographies. Lincoln Steffens, possessing one of the keenest minds among them, worked as a foreign correspondent, covering the peace-making sessions at Versailles that ended World War I; but, as far as the American public was concerned, he was virtually a forgotten man. Upton Sinclair tried to write in fiction the truths about American society that he could not deal with as fact, but he never again made anything like the impact he had in *The Jungle*—and, finally, he turned to writing a cloak-and-dagger series about an international agent, Larry Budd, entertainment novels that brought him in 1943 a Pulitzer Prize.

The upheaval of the depression brought the election of President Franklin D. Roosevelt in 1932; and, for a brief period, in a kind of knee-jerk response to disaster, there was another wave of freewheeling criticism and reform. The first years of the Roosevelt era from 1933 through 1938 brought sweeping changes. Critics again became briefly popular. Lincoln Steffens wrote his best-selling autobiography, describing the way it had been, and a flood of liberal legislation gave the nation unemployment insurance, social security, the forty-hour week, minimum wage laws, and other reforms.

Then came World War II and, swiftly following, the tensions of the Cold War era. It was a period that was conspicuous for a muted, largely uncritical and timorous press. The 1950s and 1960s—decades marked by the greatest technological and industrial revolution in history—became also decades in which the nation was smothered in a blanket of conformity; in which the critic and the dissident became suspect. They were times the old muckrakers, with their Midwestern pioneer faith in individualism, would have hated—and with reason. One has to wonder if it would have been possible in a freewheeling, muckraking age for any President of the United States to drag the nation into a disastrous war in Vietnam with hardly a ripple of responsible protest disturbing the American scene.

In the end, then, one is left with the questions Charles Edward Russell posed:

Can America long survive as a democracy without its muckrakers? Can a society in which power becomes ever more concentrated in ever fewer hands survive in freedom without its watchdogs—without muckrakers to question complacent assumptions, to cast glaring spotlights on deep-seated wrongs, to inform and arouse the public to the need for essential reforms?

That is an issue that the America of our day should both recognize and ponder well.